P9-CAD-691

MA

PHOTOGRAPHS BY
CAROL BECKWITH

TEXT BY
TEPILIT OLE SAITOTI

ASAI

HARRY N. ABRAMS, INC., PUBLISHERS, NEW YORK

Captions and Drawings by CAROL BECKWITH

Project Director: ROBERT MORTON

Editor: MARGARET DONOVAN

Designer: JOHN S. LYNCH

Library of Congress Cataloging in Publication Data

Saitoti, Tepilit Ole, 1949-
  Maasai.

  1. Maasai.
  I. Beckwith, Carol, 1945-   II. Title.
DT433.542.S22   967.6'27   79-19232
ISBN 0-8109-1303-8

Library of Congress Catalog Card Number: 79-19232

© 1980 HARRY N. ABRAMS, Inc.

Published in 1980 by Harry N. Abrams, Incorporated,
New York. All rights reserved. No part of the contents of
this book may be reproduced without the written
permission of the publishers

Printed and bound in Japan

*This book is dedicated to
the Maasai children.*

A dying Maasai elder once uttered these words:
"I have spoken and acted bravely all the time, and
I feel good about it. I hope that my children will
be able to follow in my footsteps." With these
words in mind, we have attempted to record
some of the unique customs and traditions of the
Maasai as they exist today. By revealing the
beauty and strength of the culture, we hope in
some way to help preserve it for the future.

*Tepilit Ole Saitoti
Carol Beckwith*

CONTENTS

Maasai: Land and People   17

Inkera: Youth   49

Emorata: Circumcision   77

Ilmoran: Warriors   109

Ilpayiani: Elders   181

A Personal Reflection   269

Acknowledgments   276

Maasai: Land and People

Savannah stretches endlessly
Heaven looms above
Eagle-wing clouds watch before the thunder
and lightning
Maasai young run back and forth like well-fed calves
Women always busy before the rain
Elders face the fleeing sun
Lines of cattle head home, warriors watch—
When herdsmen's chores are done, they hope for
many golden dawns.

In the contours of the Great Rift Valley of East Africa, not far from the Kenya-Tanzania border, there stands a mountain the Maasai call *Oldoinyo le Engai,* "the mountain of God." It is a lone candle, a gift from God, and thus the Maasai worship in its shadow and pray for cattle and children. Its rumbling thunder and lightning flames are nothing less than the presence and power of God, *Engai,* who is believed to live there and to whom the people bring sacrifices of lambs without spots.

As a young Maasai, I often heard the legend that, long ago, *Engai* had three children to whom he gave three gifts. The first received an arrow to make his living by hunting, the second a hoe to dig the land and grow crops, and the third a stick to use in herding cattle. This third son, whose name was Natero Kop,

was the father of the Maasai, who have since that time been the proud keepers of cattle. So, in the shadow of Mount Lengai, the Maasai have decided to observe the many sunrises and fiery sunsets and to guard their cattle grazing on the golden savannah. Standing storklike, on one leg at a time, and unconcerned, the Maasai herdsman lets time pass.

The Maasai are a pastoral people who live in Kenya and Tanzania, in the Great Rift Valley of East Africa. A cattle people who believe that all the cattle on earth belong to them, they still occasionally go on cattle raids to retrieve herds from other tribes, which they believe must have been taken from them long ago. The strong bond the Maasai have with their animals has necessitated a seminomadic way of life for them as they follow the seasons in search of grass and water for their herds.

Norman Leys, one of the first Europeans to visit the region, described the appearance of the Maasai in his book, *Kenya* (1925): "Physically they are among the handsomest of mankind, with slender bones, narrow hips and shoulders and most beautifully rounded muscles and limbs." Today there are approximately 300,000 to 400,000 Maasai, although it is difficult to take an accurate census because they dislike being counted and either hide themselves or misstate the

At left:
A Maasai elder rests in silent contemplation
within his family settlement.

numbers of their wives and children. The Maasai are increasing in numbers, but at a slower rate than the other tribes of Kenya and Tanzania. A proud people, they are struggling to retain their culture in the face of pressures to become part of the modern world.

In its strictest sense, the word *Maasai* means "speaker of the language *Maa*." There are two distinct groups of Maa-speaking peoples: those who lead a seminomadic, pastoral life—the Maasai proper and the Samburu; and those who are more settled and practice agriculture—the Baraguyu (Ilumbwa), Wa-Arusha, and Njemps. The Maasai proper tend to disapprove of the agricultural tribes, accusing them of not following all the traditional Maasai ways of life.

Maasailand is divided into approximately twelve separate geographical sections: Ilkisongo, Ilpurko, Iloitai, Ilmatapato, Iloodokilani, Ilkeekonyokie, Ilkaputiei, Ildamat, Ilsiria, Ilwuasinkishu, Ildalalekutuk, and Ilaitayiok. The largest section in Maasailand is the Ilkisongo of Tanzania, and the second largest section is the Ilpurko of Kenya. While there is some conflict between certain sections over borders, other sections get along well. In general, the size of a section is appropriate to the number of Maasai living within. The Maasai living within a particular section may belong to any one of the five clans subsequently described. Each section of Maasailand has its own name, territory, dialect, ceremonies, ways of building houses and kraals, and leadership authority.

Styles and colors of beadwork and dress also differ from section to section: for example, the Ilkisongo prefer dark red and dark blue colors in bead decoration, whereas the Ilpurko favor orange and light blue. As to differences in dress, the warriors of the Ilkisongo section wear below-the-knee togas, while the Ilpurko warriors and most Kenyan sections prefer very short togas to expose the beautiful bodies of the warriors. Laughing at the Ilkisongo, the Ilpurko warriors will say, "Such lengthy togas will trip warriors during a fight or a hunt." The Ilkisongo will respond, "You people have no decency. You walk totally naked like cows." Although the men and women of all sections make up their bodies with ocher—a special red mineral ground into powder and mixed with animal fat or water—some sections prefer a reddish-brown ocher hue, while others like a dark red. The Ilkisongo in particular dislike the deep red ocher. They will say, "Such color is similar to blood."

Differences also exist between the Tanzanian and the Kenyan Maasai. The Tanzanian Maasai have had less contact with the West and are thus more traditional than the Kenyan Maasai, who are situated closer to urban centers. The Kenyan Maasai, for

Above: *Africa, showing location of Kenya and Tanzania*

At right: *Kenya and Tanzania, showing location of Maasailand*

Below: *Sections of Maasailand (subsections and geographic landmarks in italics)*

19

example, have discarded the traditional hide dress, except for ceremonial use, and wear instead colorful factory-made fabrics. The Tanzanian Maasai, and particularly the women, still wear leather skins. Temperamentally, the Tanzanian Maasai tend to be calmer and slower than those in Kenya. In wartime they believe in slow-but-sure tactics, and at times are beaten by trying to be too sure. The Kenyans, on the other hand, believe in "Get them before they get you," and they lose at times because they rush into a situation without weighing it properly. For one short, intense, heated moment, the Kenyans will attack, hurling one weapon after another, but if the enemy is not defeated within that instant, they are left without weapons. And so they will shout, *Entomito ilmoran tooengejek* ("Save the warriors by their feet") and will speedily make their retreat.

The origins and history of the Maasai are shrouded in mystery and myth. The race is considered a hybrid between the Nilotes, a people coming from the Nile region, and the Hamites, a people originating in North Africa. One looking at Maasai dress can observe certain resemblances to the attire of the ancient Romans, who once occupied North Africa. The Maasai sword resembles the short Roman fighting sword; the warriors' hairdo follows the shape of the Roman helmet; and the toga and sandals are similar in style to those of the Romans. Linguistically, the Maasai are closest to the Bari of Sudan. They share with other groups of Nilotic origin such customs as the shaving of women's heads, the removal of the two middle teeth from the lower jaw, the one-legged stork stance, and the use of spittle in blessing. Hamitic practices among the Maasai range from circumcision and clitoridectomy in initiation rites and the age-grade system among young warriors to a dislike of eating fish and a scorn for blacksmiths. The Hamitic Nuer of Sudan also share the Maasai belief that they are the sole custodians of the earth's cattle.

It is believed that the Maasai originated in North Africa and migrated along the Nile River down to East Africa, arriving in present-day Kenya near Lake Turkana (formerly Lake Rudolf) about the fifteenth century. The story of their arrival and the extreme difficulties they encountered is the oldest memory handed down by the oral tradition of the Maasai elders:

The Maasai found themselves living in a crater-like country surrounded by a steep escarpment called Endikir Ekerio, in Kerio Valley in Kalenjin country. After a prolonged period of drought, which led to famine and deep

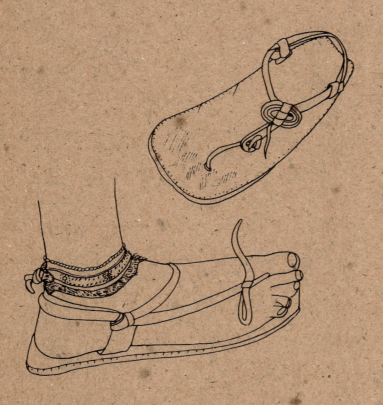

*Roman influences on Maasai appearance: sandals, hairstyle,
toga, belt, scabbard, and sword*

discouragement, the elders noticed that birds were bringing green grass to build their nests. The elders met and decided that the birds must be fetching their green grass from areas beyond the escarpment where rain had fallen, and that they would send out scouts to discover where the grass had come from. The scouts went out and, after much effort, crawling on their hands and knees, they did ascend the escarpment. When they reached the top, they found a land green and fertile and filled with sweet streams and rivers, very unlike their barren dust bowl. After exploring the new land, they gathered a few of its fruits and some green grass and returned with them as proofs of what they had seen.

The people below welcomed them back warmly and praised them for their success. The elders consulted once again on how to ascend the escarpment to the green land above it, and they decided to build a ladder to climb the treacherous ridge. After the ladder was completed, the people, with their cattle and belongings, began the ascent to the new land. Half of them had reached safety and the other half were still on the ladder, when it suddenly collapsed from the strain. Those on the ladder were thrown into the crater. After serious consultation and much deliberation, the elders decided to leave behind those stranded within the crater, since returning might jeopardize those already saved. Years later, the people left behind joined the others, but they remained different and distinct from the first group, who constitute the Maasai proper. (It is believed that those who came later are the Rendille, Pokot, and other tribes still living in Northern Kenya who bear a resemblance to the Maasai in their features and way of life.)

The first group continued on their way southward, conquering tribes in their path. They were far more organized than the other tribes they encountered and therefore were much feared. They defeated the warlike Galla tribes, the Ndorobo hunters, the powerful Sirikwa (whom they subsequently absorbed), and the Iltatua, whose wells they took over. The Bantu tribes, such as the numerous Kikuyu and Chaga, were defeated with little resistance and were pushed to the slopes of Mount Kenya and Mount Kilimanjaro.

By the end of the nineteenth century, the Maasai ranged over an area of wide, grassy plains extending 700 miles north to south, from Marsabit in present-day Northern Kenya to Kiteto at the south end of the Maasai steppe in present-day Tanzania. From east to west, their greatest range was about 200 miles, but in most places the east-west distance was much less. (Maasailand today covers a much smaller area, since land was taken during colonial times by the European settlers and has been continuously encroached upon by African agriculturalists.) Until less than a century ago, the warlike reputation of the Maasai was so respected and feared by the Bantus living in East Africa and the Arabs involved in introducing slave trade into the interior, as well as by European explorers, that Maasailand remained relatively untouched.

The Maasai's first contact with Europeans came in the late 1840s through two German members of the Church Missionary Society, a multidenominational group based in London. Dr. Ludwig Krapf encountered the Maasai living in Kenya, while Reverend John Rebmann led an expedition through Tanzania. In 1860, Dr. Krapf published a book, *Travels, Researches and Missionary Labours*, which contains probably the first written description of the Maasai and their mode of life:

> They live entirely on milk, butter, honey, and the meat of black cattle, goats and sheep...having a great distaste for agriculture, believing that the nourishment afforded by cereals enfeebles, and is only suited to the despised tribes of the mountains....When cattle fail them they make raids on the tribes which they know to be in possession of herds. They say that *Engai* (Heaven) gave them all that exists in the way of cattle and that no other nation ought to possess any....They are dreaded as warriors, laying all waste with fire and sword, so that the weaker tribes do not venture to resist them in the open field, but leave them in possession of their herds, and seek only to save themselves by the quickest possible flight.

After these initial encounters, the Maasai's reputation for fierceness slowed European efforts at exploration. In 1883–84, Joseph Thomson, sent by the British Royal Geographic Society, became the first white man to traverse Maasailand. In his book, *Through Masai Land* (1885), Thomson generally depicts the Maasai as warlike and inspiring fear, relating how he was once forced in the middle of the night to break camp to escape being killed by them. But at the same time, Thomson recognized their nobility:

> Amboseli was the country of the Masai— the warriors, the aristocrats, the lion killers, the herdsmen, the drinkers of blood and milk, and the carriers of tall spears. With profound astonishment I watched this son of the desert

as he stood before me speaking with a natural fluency and grace, a certain sense of the gravity and importance of his position and a dignity of attitude beyond all praise.

Soon after Thomson's expedition, several other explorers managed to cross Maasailand without significant opposition. Among them were Carl Peters, a German who bulldozed his way through Maasailand with modern weapons, literally shooting at every obstacle he encountered, and Count Samuel Teleki von Szek, another German, whom the Maasai still remember for his politeness and humanity.

The arrival of the Europeans in force in the late nineteenth century brought much misfortune to Maasailand. First, the late 1880s and early 1890s saw a series of natural disasters and diseases that nearly wiped out the entire race. A severe drought and famine were followed by smallpox, which was brought by the Europeans. At the same time, rinderpeste decimated the herds of the Maasai. Seeing the weakened state of the Maasai, the neighboring tribes— the Kikuyu, Kamba, and Kalenjin—attacked them to gain territory and cattle. Later, with the establishment of colonial governments in Kenya and Tanzania, the movements of the Maasai were sharply curtailed. To prevent intertribal warfare, the colonial authority forbade any of the tribes to venture beyond the territories they already occupied, and used police force and modern weapons to subdue the tribes.

But perhaps the greatest misfortune at this time was the strife among the Maasai themselves which ensued upon the death of Batiany, their *Laibon*. In Maasai society, the *Laibon* is a spiritual leader, prophet, and healer. Although his power is not political, he does have a strong say in making decisions regarding the well-being of Maasai society. The position is hereditary, handed down from father to son. The story of the quarrel between two of Batiany's sons is such a significant part of Maasai history that it must be told:

> The Maasai have a saying, "Advice given to the son of a favorite wife may be heard and acted upon by the son of an unfavored one." And so it was with two of Batiany's sons: Senteu, the eldest son of the favorite wife, and Lenana, the son of an unfavored wife.
> Batiany had grown old and sensed his death was near. In his only eye (it was believed that he was born with only one), he was losing his sight, and even his comprehension was failing. Realizing this, he called for Senteu, to whom he wanted to leave his powers of leadership, healing, prophecy, and magic. The shrewd Lenana overheard his

father calling Senteu and hid himself in a calf's pen nearby. Batiany told Senteu, "My son, I am about to sleep, and would like to leave my powers in your hands so you can lead all our people. But before I do, there are two things I want you to bring to me very early in the morning before anyone else is awake. Bring me roasted sheep meat and honey beer, and then come to my bed so I can bless you." After Senteu left the house to collect the things his father had asked for, Lenana also left and hurriedly explained to his mother what had been said. His mother thought about the situation and told her son to search for the two items and take them to his father before Senteu did. She advised him to impersonate Senteu's voice so he would receive the blessings intended for Senteu, telling him not to worry because, since they were both sons of Batiany, her husband could not undo the blessings given even if he did discover the trick.

Lenana got up at dawn ahead of everybody else, including Senteu. He collected the things demanded by his father and entered the house in which Batiany was staying. When his father asked, "Who is there?" Lenana skillfully replied, "Father, I am your eldest son, Senteu." Without hesitation his father imparted all of the arts and secrets of the *Laibon* to him. After his father had completed the blessings, he told him to leave immediately before anyone else came. On his way out of the house, Lenana met his brother Senteu, who immediately suspected that something was wrong.

Batiany heard Senteu come in and asked once again, "Who is there?" When Senteu answered, his father recognized his voice at once and asked him who had been there before. Senteu said he had passed his younger brother on his way out of the house. Then his father told him all that had happened. Batiany, much distressed, still wanted to bless his eldest son. He told him to come close so that he could embrace him and, after he did, Batiany gave him a special Maasai blessing, "Now, kiss this tongue." He continued, "What is done cannot be undone, especially as you are both my children." Finally, Batiany handed Senteu a magical box called *engidong*, which he could use to curse and cast spells on people. Although Senteu's family would multiply, Batiany said, he must accept his younger brother as spiritual leader of the Maasai.

This incident led to a feud between the two brothers which practically split the Maasai in half. The British, hoping to take advantage of the quarrel, sided with Lenana in the fight against his brother. They made him a paramount chief and restricted him to an area called Ngong, close to the government administration in Nairobi. But the plans of the British were thwarted by their lack of understanding of Maasai ways and their greed for Maasai land. They did not realize that Lenana's power was restricted by the fact that the *Laibon* is primarily a spiritual, not a political, leader. And, when the Maasai saw that the English were not content merely to administer their lands but were also interested in seizing huge tracts of land in the Rift Valley near Nakuru and in the Laikipia Plateau, they consulted together and managed to bridge their differences. Thus united, they resisted the British, but paid heavily with losses of life and cattle. When Lenana died the British finally took over this land, claiming that it was Lenana's last request.

The Maasai were very much affected by colonization. Through the biased treaties of 1904, 1911, and 1912, they lost their best territory to Europeans, including lands that had formerly been important as retreats during the dry seasons and periods of drought. Sir Charles Eliot, governor of the East Africa Protectorate from 1900 to 1904, was to initiate the first full-scale official sanction and encouragement of white settlement. The Maasai, led by Ole Gilisho and Masikonde, tried to resist, using the British law system all the way to the East Africa High Court of Appeals, but failed. Charles Eliot defended his position by saying that the Maasai not only inhabited more land than they needed, but also monopolized land that the "superior races" could develop. Although Charles Eliot had to resign because of the Maasailand issue, subsequent government authorities continued to favor the European settlers and alienate the Maasai from their land. Maasailand became a closed district; no one from other African tribes was allowed to visit without permission. Totally ignored by the colonial authority in terms of development, the Maasai are now lagging far behind most people of Tanzania and Kenya. Since gaining independence, Kenya and Tanzania have been faced with the task of helping the Maasai catch up with the rest of their nations' people.

The Great Rift Valley in which the Maasai live is itself as fascinating as Maasai history. The Rift begins in the Dead Sea, extends southward into Africa, splitting a huge part of East Africa through Ethiopia, Kenya, and Tanzania, and ends at the Indian Ocean. In an east-west direction it spreads in broken cracks from the Gulf of Aden to the Valley of the Congo, in some places stretching forty miles across. Formed in ancient times by the earth's sinking in between parallel fractures, the Rift contains the great and small lakes of Tanzania and Kenya. Its floor is open and filled with plains game. Mount Kilimanjaro, Mount Kenya, and Mount Meru, the highest mountains in East Africa, stand guard there. Once-active volcanoes have cooled down through time and are now covered with snow instead of volcanic ash, although there are still certain active volcanoes, like the one in Mount Lengai.

There are two seasons, of roughly six months each, in Maasailand: the rainy season (*alari*) and the dry season (*alamei*). The rainy season starts in November, with the short rains called *ilkisirat*, and ends in May. From May through October, the weather is dry. July and August are cold months. The pattern of Maasai life is set by the changing seasons.

When thunder and lightning break the peace, and swollen clouds let out water, the Maasai women run to seal up leaks in their houses. Soon, a blanket of green grass replaces the dry, brown one. Clear days replace the hazy ones common to the dry season. Armies of wildebeests and gazelles fill the plains and valleys; vultures swirl above the herds to look for the weak and the dead; lakes are dotted with all kinds of storks and pink flamingos. The Maasai know that it is time to move their sacred herds to the open country in the Rift Valley. They are filled with joy at the green land and the overflowing streams and lagoons, and listen with pleasure to the symphonies of frogs and crickets. The Maasai celebrate the rainy season with much singing and feasting, and many initiation ceremonies take place during this time. There is little work done except for the occasional repairing of a fence broken by bulls fighting for domination of the herd.

The dry season comes slowly but steadily. The sun scorches the land, leaving the grass dry and crackling the earth beyond belief. Cattle trails become dustier and dustier, and rocks once covered with vegetation are stripped bare. Everything in sight frowns and turns gray and dispiriting. The merciless dry season brings drought, despair, and death. Cattle weaken and die, and people also weaken as food becomes scarce. The Maasai must work harder to provide cattle—the kings and queens of life—with better pastures and water. To avoid catastrophe the herds must be moved to dry-season grazing in highland areas, where green blades of grass can be found and mountain streams can provide water. With this done, the survival of Maasailand is assured until the next dry season.

The Maasai live in harmony with the daily as well as the seasonal cycles in nature. The Maasai herder has learned to brave the bitter cold of the night and the intense heat of the day and to challenge marauding lions and cattle raiders. He uses the brightness of

Clan marks and brands

Cattle bells and amulets

the moon to guide him at night, and the celestial movement of the Milky Way foretells daybreak for him. With the dawn come the songs of women, mingled with birdsong, the first prayers of another new day. After the cows are milked, the Maasai lead their herds and flocks in different directions toward their pastures. The animals resemble beads on a string as they move in jagged lines over valleys, steppes, and rolling hills to graze together in the shadow of the mountains. Above the mountains stretches the wide horizon of the African sky, often ocean blue in color. On certain days, rolling clouds cast huge shadows which glide over the trees, distant hills, and stretches of open country. Bearing fog and mist, these clouds make their way to the highlands and blanket the mountains protectively for days at a time, making them invisible to the eyes of anxious travelers. The fog and mist stimulate the growth of moss and fern, leaving the bearded pillar trees soaking and dripping.

The Maasai's harmony with nature is closely entwined with their reverence for God. The Maasai believe in one God, *Engai*, who dwells both on earth and in heaven. *Engai* is the Supreme God, and no one else can be called by that name. There are two aspects to God: *Engai Narok*, the God which is black, the good and benevolent God; and *Engai Na-nyokie*, the red or avenging God, which is an aspect of God's holy anger. The black God is seen in thunder and rain, which bring grass to the cattle and prosperity to the Maasai; the red God is expressed in violent lightning, which can strike and kill, and in the extreme dry season, which brings famine and death. To the Maasai, God is the master of both life and death.

Although the Maasai pray as a community during major ceremonies, their daily life also incorporates many phrases expressing their awareness of God's presence. Individuals may be heard murmuring such words as *Engai tajapaki tooinaipuko inono* ("God, shield me with your wings") or *Engai ake naiyiolo* ("Only God knows"). A Maasai who thinks he has been mistreated by fate or by a more powerful individual will say, *Tapala amoo etii ake Engai* ("Never mind, because God is still present"). Some Maasai prayers refer to God as male, others as female. One song praises *Naamoni aiyai*, "The She to whom I pray," while another addresses *Olasera ingumok*, "He of many colors." To the Maasai, God's greatness encompasses all attributes.

The two most important things that the Maasai constantly pray for are children and cattle. When two people meet, they exchange the greeting, *Keserian ingera? Keserian ingishu?* ("How are the children? How are the cattle?"). Cattle are very special in Maasailand,

and in fact form the basis of the entire culture, being the main form of sustenance, wealth, and power. A recent census estimates the cattle population of Maasailand at three million, more cattle per person than found in any other tribe in Africa. The Maasai also keep sheep and goats, which they consider of economic value and use for food and in ceremonies.

A person of modest wealth will have a herd of about fifty head of cattle. (This number is considered *ingishu naadaari*, that is, large enough to graze securely.) The larger the herd, the richer the person, and a Maasai may have as many as a thousand in his herd. Without children, however, he is not considered truly wealthy. *Arkasis*, the term for a rich man, applies only to one blessed with both cattle and children. A man with less than fifty cows feels poor, and the following song illustrates his unwillingness to remain in this state:

> *Abuaki emutii iyai endarona nabuaki alapa elepo. Peemejo*
> *Engai nemejo engop kalo ele lembwaak ebwaki. Nanu*
> *naibeloiye emurt osenaa looingishu naitongor engonom.*
> *Atayewo olaingoni sambu emurut loongishu elekai supuko*
> *nanang'ie.*

> I pray to evening and I pray to dawn and I pray to the moonrise, so that God and earth may not say, "Who is this who never prays while others are praying?" I, whose misery weighs heavily on my neck with a herd of less than fifty. I want a bull with stripes on his neck from another country to add to my herd.

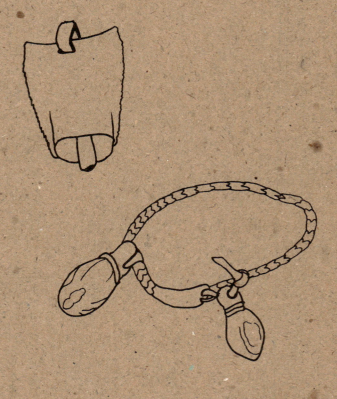

The clans or family trees of Maasailand are believed to have their origin in the ownership of cattle. There are two major pillars or totems of Maasai society—*Oodo Mongi*, the Red Cow, and *Orok Kiteng*, the Black Cow—and these two are further subdivided into five clans. The story is told that, in the early days of the Maasai, Natero Kop married two wives. To one he gave red cows, and she built her house on the right-hand side of her husband's gate to the kraal; the other was given black cows and occupied the left-hand side. Each of the wives was named according to the color of her cows. The first wife, Nado Mongi (the Red Cow), gave birth to three children: Lelian, who founded Ilmolelian clan; Lokesen, who founded Ilmakesen clan; and Losero, the founder of Iltaarrosero. These three clans form the right-hand pillar of Maasai clans. The second wife, named Narok Kiteng (the Black Cow), gave birth to two sons: Naiser, the original ancestor of Ilaiser clan, and Lukum, the father-founder of Ilukumae. These two clans are the left-hand pillar of the Maasai clans. The Ilmolelian and Ilaiser clans are the most prominent and powerful among the Maasai, and so it is thought that they must have been founded by the eldest sons of each of the two pillars.

Within the five Maasai clans the members know which families may or may not intermarry. It is recommended that the right pillar should marry the left pillar, but if marriage does occur within one pillar of clans, the prospective husband may pay a heifer to the family of his bride to wipe out the incest. When a man and woman have children, their offspring assume the clan of the father.

For each clan there is one principal mark or brand, and all the cattle belonging to the various families within the clan are branded in the same special way. In addition to the principal brand for the whole clan there is a special brand, usually smaller, by which the actual owner can be recognized. Besides branding, each family has a special method of slitting the ears of their animals. For cattle, one ear is slit to represent the totem to which the owner belongs and the other ear is slit to represent his clan; the ears of sheep and donkeys may be slit as the owner wishes. If a lost cow is seen, it can be recognized as belonging to the Ilaiser clan and also to such and such a person. One has only to see cattle grazing anywhere in Maasailand to be able to tell, by the brand or earmark, whether or not the owner is one's relative.

A herd is composed of cows, bulls, and oxen. In a herd of fifty cows there may be two or three bulls, usually one big, one medium, and one small. The number of bulls is restricted and their ages are kept different in order to prevent fighting. At an early age, the rest of the males are castrated into oxen to be used for meat or sold, either for money or in exchange. The Maasai select which bulls to leave uncastrated on the basis of certain desirable characteristics of the father and mother. For example, the mother must have lots of milk and beautiful colors, and the father a large size and strength. Some families, such as the *Laibon* family, prefer bulls with large horns to add to the beauty of the herd.

A family's cattle are personally known and loved, the way one loves one's child. The temperament of each animal and even its particular voice are recognized. While still young, a Maasai is taught how to sing to the cattle, to describe their horn formations, humps, and colors, and their little individual peculiarities. Many Maasai songs are concerned with cattle. The one below was sung by a young woman to the warrior she loved:

Mee osingolio kisiaje nemee engopiro natii elpapit, kisiaje ilooitong' oseroo laalaram onaree irrepeta.

It was not your dancing nor the feather in your hair that attracted me, but rather your big herd of cattle which tramples the bush and clears forest passes. It is this which deserves praise.

Cattle also supply milk—the staple of the Maasai diet—which the people consume fresh or in a sour, yogurt form. Babies are given ghee, another dairy product, similar to clarified butter. Rarely is an animal slaughtered for its meat, except on such special occasions as when a woman gives birth, when a person is very sick, when warriors go on retreats to gain strength, or when a major ceremony takes place. Most food is shared in the Maasai community, and when one kills a cow, everyone who prefers to eat meat that day will join in. However, milk and meat must not be eaten at the same time since it is believed that mixing the two will give tapeworms to people or cause their cows to be cursed with swollen udders. Beyond health considerations, the Maasai feel that it is a betrayal of the animal to feed on it alive, by drinking its milk, and also to feed on it dead, by eating its meat. So a Maasai must decide which of the two he or she will do that day.

The Maasai drink blood during the dry season when they run short of milk. The animal is not killed in obtaining the blood, but rather the tip of an arrow is used to make an incision in its jugular vein. Warriors often drink the blood of healthy animals with the belief that it will give them strength. When a woman gives birth, when a person is wounded, or when a boy or girl is circumcised, he or she is given blood to replace the lost blood. In recent years, the custom of blood drinking has partially given way to the consumption of a cereal made by mixing cornmeal and water.

The Maasai utilize every part of their cattle. Besides drinking the animal's milk and blood and eating its meat, the Maasai use its urine for medicinal purposes and to wash calabashes; its dung to cover and seal their houses; its horns to make containers; its hoofs for ornaments such as rings; and its hides for clothing, shoes, house and bed coverings, and ropes. No ceremony can be performed without including a cow, bull, or ox in one way or another. It is through their cattle that the Maasai have attained self-sufficiency. It is no wonder, then, that they consider little in the world to be of equal value.

Even the structure of the Maasai settlement is purposely designed for the protection of cattle. When several families decide to live together, they establish a settlement called an *engang*, or kraal, for themselves and their animals. As a boundary for the kraal and to keep out predators, the men build a circular fence from the prickly branches of thornbushes or from long

Calabash with two cleaning brushes

poles tied together. The fence may be of varying thicknesses and security depending on how dangerous the surrounding area is. Inside the fence, along its perimeter, the women build igloo-shaped houses of branches and grass, and then seal them over with a thick layer of cow dung for warmth and for dryness during the rainy season. They leave a large open space in the center of the kraal into which the cattle are driven at night for protection against predators and cattle thieves. Kraals are built at good distances from one another to avoid cattle from one kraal mixing with those from another.

The Maasai love grass because their cattle feed on it. If there is drought, the women fasten grass onto their clothes and go to offer prayers to God, so that rain might fall. If a warrior is beating a boy on the grazing ground, the boy tears up some grass and shouts, "Green grass, green grass, I beg you," and when the warrior sees that the boy has grass in his hand he stops. Again, if the Maasai fight with an enemy and then wish to make peace, they hold out some grass as a gesture. Should one man ask forgiveness of another with grass in his hand and his request be not attended to, it is said that the man who refuses to listen is a Ndorobo (a man from a tribe with no cattle, despised by the Maasai) and that he does not know about cattle. For the Maasai say, "God gave us cattle and grass—without grass there are no cattle, and without cattle there are no Maasai."

The life of a Maasai male is a well-ordered progression through a series of life-stages, which are determined by age, initiated through ceremonies, and marked by specific duties and privileges. The males of every Maasai section pass through three main stages: boyhood, warriorhood, and elderhood. Warriors are subdivided into junior and senior warriors and together form one generation or age-set. Approximately every fifteen years, a new generation of warriors comes of age. Each generation of warriors is given its own name, for example, *Iltobola* ("Those who grow and prosper"), as a symbolic wish or blessing to live up to. When the warriors graduate into elderhood, they are replaced by another generation of warriors. Elders progress through junior and then senior elderhood, and eventually become ancient elders, who, because of their old age, retire from the active direction of Maasai affairs.

While there are superficial differences among sections, the Maasai are unified at the core by their passage through these age-sets and by the performance of four major ceremonies, each of which initiates a new life-stage. These four major ceremonies, performed by all Maasai males, are:

Alamal Lengipaata, the ceremony boys undertake
   just before circumcision;
Emorata, the circumcision ceremony, which
   initiates them into warriorhood;
Eunoto, the graduation of warriors into elderhood;
Olngesherr, the confirmation of total elderhood.

The four ceremonies have certain features in
common: ritual head shaving, continual blessings,
the slaughter of an animal, ceremonial painting of the
face or body, singing, dancing, and feasting. The
ceremonies are performed section by section. For
reasons unknown, *Olngesherr* must first be performed
by the Ilkisongo and then by the other sections. *Alamal
Lengipaata* must be opened up by the Ilkeekonyokie
section in order for the other sections to follow.

The following chapters will trace the patterns of
traditional Maasai life from birth through childhood,
maturity, and elderhood, detailing some of the rituals
that signify each life-stage. Through their long and
difficult history, the Maasai have fought to maintain
this traditional way of life. Today, however, they can
no longer resist the pressures of the modern world.
The survival of Maasai culture has ceased to be a
question; in truth, it is rapidly disappearing. And so,
the sweetness, pride, and beauty of the life portrayed
here take on an added poignancy as they vanish, like
the mists over the mountains of Maasailand.

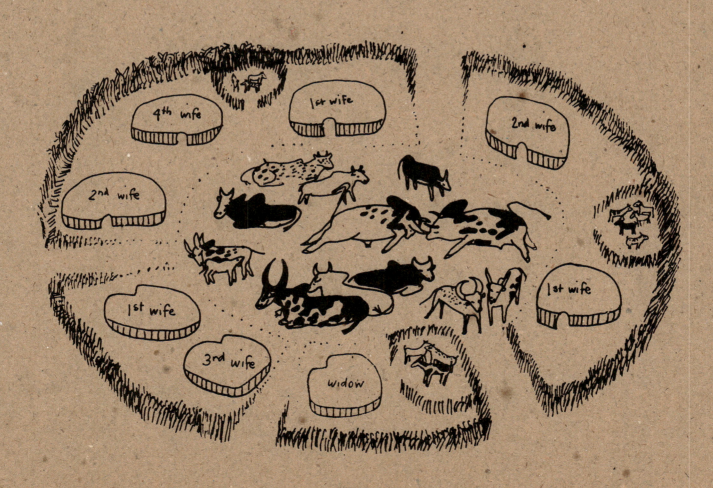

A Maasai settlement (engang)

In the land where the Maasai live,
the Great Rift Valley of Kenya and Tanzania,
thorny acacia trees punctuate the grassy savannah;
broad lakes, meandering rivers, and flat, seasonally
parched lowlands rise toward softly rolling green hills.
Distant mountains, with names that ring with magic—
Kilimanjaro, Kenya, Meru, Lengai—stand like
sentinels, defining the region; an intense equatorial
light shines everywhere. The air is fragrant with
leleshwa leaves; the plain teems with herds of grazing
zebras, antelope, and wildebeestes; the scrubby forest
echoes with the crash of elephants. Moving their cattle,
families, and possessions, the Maasai follow the
growing of the grass as precious rain soaks the
earth. They live as they always have, nomads
but not without a home.

Opposite: Mount Kilimanjaro   *Above:* Olduvai Gorge   *Below:* Lake Eyasi

The Maasai build settlements called *engangs*, or kraals—
circular enclosures containing dung-plastered houses.

Inkera: Youth

"May God give you children, may God give you cattle." In Maasai prayers, the two are never separate. If a Maasai has children, he will need cattle to feed and clothe them; if he has cattle, he will want children to herd and care for them. Children and cattle, therefore, complement each other, but if he had to choose between the two, a Maasai would prefer children. There are two reasons for this, one emotional, one practical. First, Maasai adore children. One often hears a devoted parent affectionately calling "my soft umbilical cord," "my fragile bones," or "child of my beloved man." And, too, after reasoning it out, the Maasai has concluded that a man with many children and no cattle is far richer than one in the opposite situation. If he has daughters, they will marry, and the dowry paid by the husband-to-be will include cattle. If he has sons, they will become warriors and capture cattle during their raids. Either way, children will lead to owning cattle. So, they come first, although the Maasai thinks having to choose is unfair—he would rather have both.

A Maasai woman in the early stages of pregnancy develops a strong liking for certain foods. With the first signs of pregnancy, she will shyly ask her husband or relatives for some favorite food, perhaps sheep meat, goat, cow, or even wild animal meat. This demand must be met because it is believed that if it is not, the woman may have a miscarriage. In the later stages of pregnancy, the expectant mother selects what she eats carefully. She eats less food, drinks more water, and refrains from eating certain specified foods. Fresh milk, for instance, is forbidden because it is thought to fatten the baby and thus make the delivery more dangerous. The mother-to-be must not eat the meat of any animal that has died of disease, but instead should consume only parts of healthy animals that have been properly slaughtered. The meat she eats must be thoroughly cooked to remove any possibility of parasites and traces of juice, believed to fatten the mother and baby. Dried meat is favored. Vomiting, induced by the use of special roots and herbs, is prescribed. The purpose of the constant water drinking and the induced vomiting is to clean the expectant mother's stomach, purify her bloodstream, and keep her healthy. The main point of all these dietary laws is to restrict fattening foods as much as possible, since the Maasai believe that excess weight, of either the mother or the unborn infant, will make the process of birth difficult and dangerous.

Maasai babies come into the world in the midst of busy women crying, "Hold here, lift there, push hard." The birth of a baby takes place in the expectant mother's house, with a midwife in attendance. Midwives tend to be experienced mothers known to

At left:
Eager for one more taste, a Maasai
child overturns a cooking pot.

be serious and careful, usually coming from the family of the expectant mother. If there is no member of the family able to fulfill this role, the family will bring in an outside expert a month or two ahead of time to avoid surprises in case the baby arrives earlier than expected. Besides delivering the baby, the midwife is responsible for severing the umbilical cord. As she does this she pronounces the words, "You are now responsible for your life, as I am responsible for mine." This symbolic utterance is to invite the newborn to our harsh environment, which is so different from the softness and warmth of the womb. It also marks the separation of the mother and child—now each one has a life of its own.

Once the afterbirth is thrown away, the mother and infant are cleaned with a mixture of water and milk. The sex of the child is very important, and the father, who is not allowed near the house during delivery, must be told it as soon as possible. If the baby is a boy, the midwife tells the father to draw blood from the jugular vein of a bullock and to make a mock attempt to draw blood from a heifer. The procedure is reversed when a girl is born. The blood is collected in a calabash, by a male if the baby is a boy and by a female if it is a girl. By watching these proceedings, all present will know the sex of the newborn child. A drink is then made by mixing the blood drawn from the bullock or heifer with some warm milk, and this is given to the mother to drink. Inside the house in which the delivery has taken place, a ram known as the *olkipoket* ("house purifier") is slaughtered, and its meat is consumed solely by the women of the village, who have gathered inside and brought milk to the mother as a present.

Soon after the women have eaten the meat, they sing prayer songs. One popular song is *Naomoni Aaayai:*

Naomoni aaayai.
The one who is prayed for and I also pray.
Naikurukur nesha,
God of the thunder and the rain,
Iye oshi ak-aaomon.
Thee I always pray.
Kileken oilepu,
Morning star which rises,
Iye oshi ak-aaomon.
Thee I always pray.
Paasai leleshwa,
The Indescribable Color,
Iye oshi ak-aaomon.
Thee I always pray.

This song constitutes a blessing to the house, the mother, the infant, and the whole family to whom the child is born. The following day, another plump sheep is slaughtered for its fat, which must be melted and given to the mother to drink. The meat of this sheep may be eaten by both men and women, but the midwife must be given the best cuts of the rump meat.

From that day on, the family is free to provide the mother with any kind of food she likes, but it must be high in fat content, to build her strength and health. The mother breast-feeds the baby for two or three months, after which her milk is supplemented with cow's milk and ghee. The infant is fed whenever it cries and not on schedule.

The age at which the baby is named differs from family to family. Certain families give a first name when the baby is still very young. At the first naming ceremony, both the baby and its mother have their heads shaved, and a lamb is slaughtered. Between the ages of eight and twelve, the child is given a second name which is added to the name given at birth. At the second naming ceremony, some families butcher a bullock, and its hide is skinned and tanned with the tail intact. This skin is kept by the child's family, who value it as a token of the ceremony.

Both naming ceremonies are usually very colorful. The mother puts on her best clothes—of soft lambskin or goatskin stitched with beads—her many bead necklaces and earrings, and a heavy ocher make-up. The elders and women participate in the naming of the child. After they decide which name to give the child, they bless it, saying "May that name dwell in you." The child's family and the guests reply *Naaii* ("Yes, Lord"). On the evening of the ceremony and on the one following, the child's mother closes the entrance to the kraal by blocking it with specially cut branches, bearing green leaves, from a sacred tree such as the African olive or cordia ovalis. She also removes the branches from the entrance in the morning before the herds leave the kraal.

The baby is cared for mainly by its mother and her daughters, if she happens to have any, and by the grandmothers of the community. They show affection for the child by smiling and tickling it, dancing with it, raising it high up in the air the way Maasai warriors dance. The mother sings to the child:

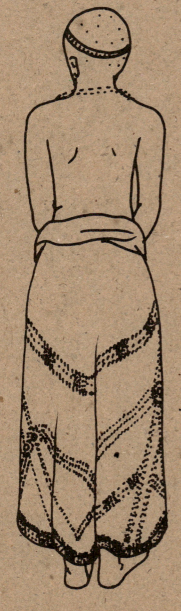

Beaded lambskin skirt

> *Engonyakonya,*
> Grow up, my child,
> *Yawa ingik aulo.*
> Grow up like a mountain.
> *Tabana Komerek,*
> Equal Mount Meru,
> *Tabana Oldoinyo Keri,*
> Equal Mount Kenya,

Tabana Oldoinyo Oibor.
Equal Kilimanjaro.
Tanapa minyi o ng'utunyi.
Help your mother and father.

While the child is still young and just learning to walk, the woman caring for it will hold both its hands to help with its first steps and will sing:

Tadotu dotu enginyi aaayai,
Walk, walk, walk, my little one,
Tadotu dotu enginyi aaayai.
Let us walk, my little one.
Mapeepe teteyai mapeepe teteyai.
Slowly, let us walk slowly.

During the early stages of walking and talking, the child mingles freely with everyone in the family. At about three or four years of age, however, the boys are encouraged to associate more with men, and the girls with women. Both are still basically looked after by women.

In Maasai villages, one often sees a boy of three or four holding a stick, which first only symbolizes his future as a herder but later is used in actually learning how to herd cattle. This is soon joined by a second, taller stick with a sharp point to represent a warrior's spear, for at this age a boy starts to aspire to be a warrior. There are frequent injuries inflicted from those spearlike sticks.

Singing becomes more and more important to children as they grow up. They sing such songs as:

Eetwo engi shwang,
Our cattle have come,
Olaram muje,
But instead of going out to honor them,
Narom telusie nemapung'oki.
I peer through a small opening.

("A small opening" might refer either to the hole in the wall of a Maasai house, which lets in air and light, or to a chink in the fence surrounding the kraal.)

The children also become conscious of the dangers to Maasailand. If, for instance, there is drought, they will have no milk. So they sing the following song during the dry season:

Engai, taasha
God, let rain fall
Maagorr esuate
So that I do not choke
Olnjoni musana
On the tough meat of the old hide

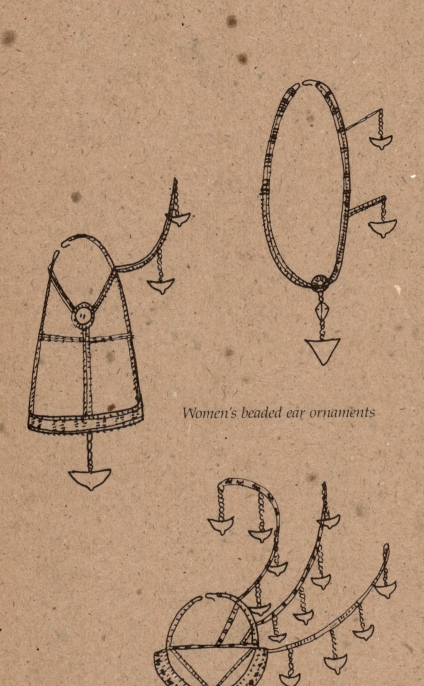

Women's beaded ear ornaments

Oorieki enguruon
Which is used to take away ashes
Lengaji oloiboni.
From the *Laibon's* house.

Like all children, Maasai boys and girls love to
play. The boys construct miniature kraals out of earth,
dung, or stones and place pebbles or berries inside
them to represent sheep and cattle. Young girls play
with dolls made from mud or with jacks made from
stones or berries. Boys and girls sometimes play
together, their favorite games being hide-and-seek and
playing grownups.

Molding the children's characters is a communal
activity. While still young, children are given some
minor chores like herding lambs, goat-kids, and
calves, but they are not seriously reprimanded if
they neglect them. They soon learn, however, to
distinguish what is bad from what is good. They are
encouraged to behave well in the presence of elders or
anyone older who might render punishment, for
anyone in the community may punish a child who has
done wrong. Punishment might take the form of a
verbal rebuff or a spanking. On the other hand, a child
who performs good deeds, such as taking proper care
of the lambs or goat-kids or helping anyone in the
community, will be rewarded, perhaps by some milk
or a good piece of meat.

Respect is taught early in life in Maasailand. The
child is taught to call all elders "Father" and all women
"Mother." Sometimes children address adults by
the name of their offspring, for example, *Koto Meto*,
the mother of Meto. Calling all elders "Father" is
sometimes confusing. If there is a group of elders
seated together, they will always ask, "Which one?"
and the child is forced to point out the elder he is
addressing.

When the child is four or five years old, an
experienced elder woman removes its two lower
incisors. Aside from enhancing beauty, this makes it
possible to feed the child through the small opening
should it get sick from tetanus and not be able to
open its mouth. After the second set of teeth grows in,
they are removed once again. Between the ages
of five and seven, girls undertake certain domestic
responsibilities like helping their mothers by collecting
firewood and cleaning calabashes. Young boys at this
age look after older calves and may even accompany
an older person herding cattle.

Between seven and eight years of age, both males
and females have the upper part of their right ear
pierced and, when that is healed, the left ear is also
pierced in the same spot. In a year or two, a bigger
hole is pierced in the lobe of the right ear and then in

53

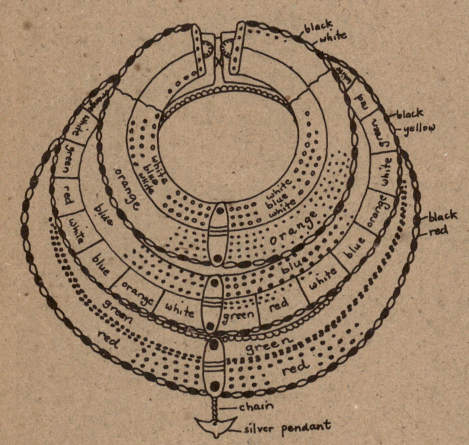

black
white
black
yellow
black
red
chain
silver pendant

The colors of a typical beaded necklace

the left lobe. Wooden plugs or wads of leaves are inserted in the lobes to increase their sizes. The larger the earlobe, the more beautiful to the Maasai. When a child is grown he or she may choose to have decorative patterns, called *ilkigerot*, marked onto the chest or stomach by burning or incision with a knife. This is not mandatory, however, and depends on whether one thinks they enhance physical beauty.

From seven to nine years of age, the child learns and joins in many games played by its mates. One such game is called *engilaut* and involves jumping over a horizontal stick held by two children and gradually raised in height. They also enjoy throwing cattle dung at each other. In the evening they play warriors and lions, pretending that a lion has attacked the herd and they are warriors in pursuit.

Girls between nine and twelve years old begin to associate more with the warriors and less with the younger boys. This is a time when they may select boyfriends from among the warriors and may even begin to have lovers if they want to. The girls sing together and compose love songs to their warrior boyfriends. They adorn themselves with beautiful necklaces and soft hides, both decorated with glass beads bought from traders coming to Maasailand. Usually each girl or woman makes her own necklaces, using wire or sinew as thread and following the current fashions. In order to bead a skin, a wire is sharpened into a fine point and attached to a small stick to make a needle. This needle is used to puncture holes in the cured hide. A sinew made into a thread is then strung with beads and pushed through the holes to form decorative patterns on the hide. At this age, girls also milk cows, draw water, collect firewood, plaster the house, and even tend sheep and calves if their fathers have no boys.

The games of big boys, between nine and twelve, change in character. Although they are basically the same games as before, they get rougher and tougher. Most games take place at night, under a bright moon, in the center of the kraal. This adds to their danger since the boys are surrounded by sleeping herds that could stampede at any moment and crush them. During dark nights, without the moonlight, both boys and girls gather indoors to listen to the stories and legends of the old days.

All storytelling among the Maasai takes place at night, because they believe that to tell stories during the daytime would be to risk losing their cattle. When all the cattle are secured, the calves, goats, and kids put in separate pens, and everyone has eaten, the children seek out the house of a woman who is a good storyteller. There they sit for hours before an amber-colored fire listening to stories and tales like this one:

One day, Natero Kop, the beginner of the earth, instructed the Maasai patriarch Leeyo that if a child of the tribe were to die, he was to cast away the body and say, "Man, die and come back again. Moon, die and remain away." Since the next child to die was not his own, Leeyo did not bother to obey. When it came time to remove the body, he picked it up and said to himself, "This child is not mine. When I cast it away I shall say, 'Man, die and remain away. Moon, die and return.'" So he spoke those words and returned home. The next child to die was one of Leeyo's own, and when he cast away its body, he followed Natero Kop's instructions and said, "Man, die and return. Moon, die and remain away." But Natero Kop told him, "It is of no use now, for you spoilt matters with the other child." This is how it came about that when a man dies, he does not return, whilst when the moon dies, it comes back again and is always visible to us.

There are many different legends handed down through oral tradition concerning the origin of the Maasai. The following version of how the Maasai came to be is a popular story:

When Leeyo grew old and lay dying, he called his two sons to his side and said to them, "My children, I am now very old. I wish to bid you goodbye." Leeyo then asked his elder son what he wanted out of all his wealth. The son replied, "I want something of all the things upon the earth—some cattle, a few goats and sheep, and some of the earth's food."

"Since you want something of all the earth's things," the old man said, "take a few herds of cattle, a few goats and sheep, and some of the food of the earth, for that is a large number of things." The elder son replied, "Very well."

Leeyo then called his younger son and asked him what he wanted. "I should like, Father," the younger one said, "the fan that you carry suspended from your arm, as a remembrance of you." Leeyo was so touched by his son's modesty that he blessed him and told him, "My child, because you have chosen this fan, God will give you wealth, and you will be great among your brother's people."

And so it came to pass that the elder son got a little of everything on earth. His descendants became the numerous Bantu farmers, who both grow crops and keep a few animals. The younger son's descendants became the ancestors of today's proud Maasai.

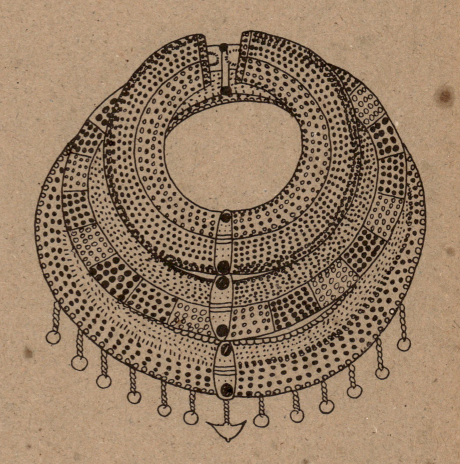

When the children have had enough of storytelling, they will often choose to play one of the many Maasai indoor games that do not require much bodily exercise. In *olengukuo*, for instance, one person hides a piece of charcoal in one of his hands and makes the others guess which hand it is in. When another player succeeds in guessing the correct hand, he takes over the charcoal. Another hand game is the one called *osiaj*, in which one person is designated "even" and the other "odd." The two players sit facing each other and each person grabs either his own right or left arm. If both persons hold the same arm, the person who is "even" wins. If they hold opposite arms, the person designated "odd" wins.

But the most exciting and complex game of all is *eloiyetia*, the Maasai riddle. Here are several examples:

Q: Tell me four great wonders.
A: (a) A calabash, which does not drink the milk it contains.
   (b) A snake, which moves without legs.
   (c) Water, which, though having no legs, still travels.
   (d) A stool, which has legs and yet does not walk.

Q: I have many warriors but all stand on one leg. What do they resemble?
A: The *Euphorbia candelabra* tree.

Q: What does your mother resemble if she is long yet does not reach up to a sheep's udder?
A: The road.

Q: Your mother uses abusive language while passing through the center of the kraal. What does she resemble?
A: A woman chewing gum. ["Gum" here refers to a natural substance the Maasai make from a tree resin.]

Q: What is the paramount thing in a man's life?
A: The stomach.

Q: How many types of trees do you have in your country?
A: Two, the dry ones and the green ones.

Q: What object can never be overtaken?
A: One's shadow.

When boys and girls reach puberty in Maasailand, their thoughts increasingly turn to the time when they will be promoted to adulthood. They spend countless hours checking whether their pubic hair has grown, and will say, "The hair is there, but is visible only in the sun." Adolescents will fight among themselves

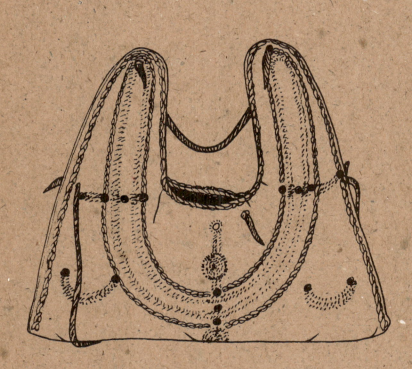

Olbene, a bag for a woman's necklaces and bracelets

with sticks or ropes, away from the elders, women, and warriors. These big boys and girls also cause many fights among the younger children. They will set one against the other and then sit on the sidelines and enjoy the fight. Also during this time the dogs of the kraal, which are kept to scare away hyenas and protect the herds, are given terrible beatings by the boys when they steal food or otherwise misbehave.

In every way, the status of uncircumcised boys in Maasailand makes them yearn to be warriors. Even when they have grown up enough to undertake important responsibilities like moving cattle to new pastures far from the main kraals, the boys are not allowed to dress like the warriors, to put colorful ornaments in their pierced earlobes, or to carry the tall spear of the warrior. Rather, they wear a plain toga with few and simple ornaments and no ocher make-up, and carry a spear with a short blade. Although they are forbidden to have sex or even to glance at the warriors' girl friends, they will often try to sneak at night to visit the girls.

Uncircumcised adolescent girls date warriors steadily and go to their manyattas with them. The girls become a source of pride and legend to the warriors who love them. You will hear warriors swearing on their names, such as when a warrior drops something, he will say "I love Tikako." Even during one of the highest moments of Maasai manhood, when a warrior is killing a lion, he will call out the name of a girl he loves as well as his father's name.

Adolescence is also the time when a girl, with the help of her mother, will learn and master all the duties of womanhood. Cooking, sewing, cleaning house, taking care of babies, the young girl continually helps her mother in whatever she does. If the girl has no brothers to tend the cattle, she will be obliged to perform the task, but this line of duty is disliked by girls. Girls between twelve and sixteen may decorate the upper part of their ears with beaded earrings and wear elaborate necklaces, but they are not allowed to decorate their lower earlobes or to wear the long metal chain (*emonyorit*) and coiled brass ornaments (*isurutia*) worn by older women.

Uncircumcised boys do not hold councils unless specially authorized by the warriors. If they are seen gathering together without permission, they will be beaten and dispersed. Warriors and youths do not get along well, and warriors are always happy to find some reason to give boys a beating. When a boy is beaten by the warriors, he is not allowed to fight back. If he does, all the boys in the area will be severely punished.

The boys at this age spend practically all their time looking after cattle. At certain times, the boys will play sick so they can rest, but such tricks are futile because if the warriors suspect they are pretending they will prescribe for them the most bitter-tasting medicine. The boys often find it better to continue to work than to drink such medicine.

The adolescent boy contributes enormously to the well-being of the herd. As a Maasai son, he has been brought up to regard cattle not merely as wealth but as an extension of himself, and has been taught the importance of learning all he can about the herd. For instance, a youth with a sharp Maasai eye will be able to tell when an animal is sick by observing the appearance of its hide. He can also diagnose the disease by looking for certain symptoms, such as the swelling of lymphatic glands if it is East Coast fever. He will then separate the sick animal from the rest of the herd to avoid spreading the disease, and will take measures to cure it.

The Maasai youth must also be able to tell if cattle are missing from the herd, not by counting them the way one counts money, but by knowing they are gone the way one would miss an absent friend. From his own experiences during long herding days, the boy's father will have told him the structure of the herd—which animals are always in the rear, which prefer the flanks, and which are always in the front. In searching for missing animals, the herder must first look to the rear or the flanks. Animals in the rear are most likely to lag behind and get lost; the rear and also the flank animals are most vulnerable to predators.

The boy is taught how important it is for herders to remain alert and that, in bush areas, it is even possible to lose the whole herd if one falls asleep. Keeping vigilant will also enable the boy to report accurately when he last saw an animal if one does happen to stray and to help those who will be searching for the animal. Any Maasai herder who loses track of his herd is always reprimanded, but a youth who does will be physically beaten. (It's a big embarrassment for any grown-up person to lose cattle. Most grownups, both warriors and elders, seldom sit down when they are herding to avoid the shame of losing cattle.)

A Maasai youth learning to herd must also know how to protect his animals from predators. An elder will make sure that his son can recognize most enemies to the cattle, such as hyenas, leopards, and, of course, lions. He must be able to identify their tracks, distinguish their sounds, and know how to approach them quietly to avoid being seen. The youth will learn to study the trails of both cattle and wild animals and to find out which wild animals have passed before the cattle pass over the marks. An elder will ask his son such questions as, "What wild animal

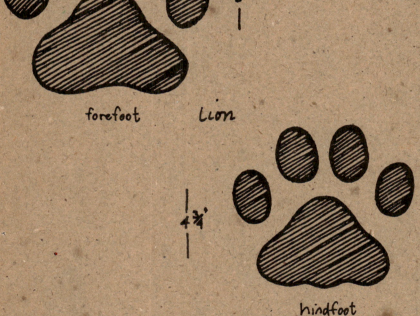

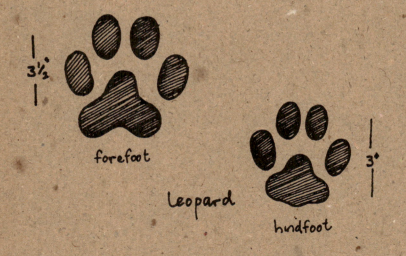

Cheetah, lion, and leopard paw prints

droppings excite cattle when they see or smell them?" and the son will answer, "Lions and ostriches." If the herd is attacked and the youth cannot defend it adequately by himself, he is told that he must rush home as quickly as possible to report the danger. His special alarm call is sure to be speedily answered by the warriors, the protectors of Maasailand.

When they reach the age of sixteen, boys throughout Maasailand become increasingly insistent that they are ready to become adults through the ceremony of circumcision. To demonstrate that they are fully grown and able to take over from the aging warriors the task of protecting Maasailand, the youths engage in a great deal of hunting of dangerous animals. In groups and individually, armed with spears only, the boys track and kill buffalo, elephants, rhinoceros, and lions. Having thus proved that they are strong, dependable, and confident of protecting Maasailand, they speak to the junior elders, who will act as their sponsors at the circumcision ceremony and are therefore called the fire-stick elders, that is, those who will kindle the fire on circumcision day. The youths ask the elders to approach the *Laibon* and request that a new circumcision period be opened. The elders decide whether a new set of warriors is needed to replace the old and whether the eligible boys form a group large enough to defend Maasailand adequately.

If permission is given, a ceremony called *Embolata Olkiteng* ("holding the bullock by the horns") is then performed, but only by one section of the Maasai, the Ilkeekonyokie. In this ceremony, the boys further demonstrate their strength and maturity by capturing a bullock by its horns and wrestling the animal to the ground with only their bare hands. The performance of this ceremony by the Ilkeekonyokie will open a new circumcision period, lasting from three to four years, in all the other Maasai sections.

Embolata Olkiteng is followed by the ceremony called *Alamal Lengipaata*, which is performed everywhere and immediately precedes the youths' formal initiation into manhood. In this ceremony the boys select a *Laibon* from their fathers' generation to help them in making the important decisions which will affect their future. The *Laibon* gives them a new generation-name in the place of *ilayok* ("youth"), the name they have been commonly known by, and blesses them to prosper. All the boys circumcised during this period will carry the new name of their generation throughout warriorhood. When they graduate to elderhood, they will be given another generation-name in place of the one given at *Alamal Lengipaata*.

Alamal Lengipaata begins with a peaceful

procession of well-dressed youths, adorned with the warriors' ornaments which they have always longed for, such as ochered hair and ostrich feather headdresses, and accompanied by the warriors' girl friends. The boys' bodies are decorated with the chalk-white paint called *enturoto*. After the procession, the boys leave the kraal to spend a night out in the open. They camp under the stars, near a neighboring body of water, without a fence or spears to protect them. There is much singing and celebrating throughout the night and continual blessings by the *Laibon* and elders, who have gathered to officiate at the ceremony.

At this stage on their road to manhood, the youths are allowed to hold councils, discuss matters collectively, and make decisions with the help of the fire-stick elders. They consider seriously what are the acceptable norms of behavior for the impending stage of warriorhood. Soon after the boys are permitted to hold council and as they near circumcision, they elect from among themselves an *Alaigwanani*. This boy will preside over all the future meetings they hold, will represent the group in any discussions with their circumcision sponsors, and will bring back ideas and suggestions from the sponsors. The boys elect this one boy on the grounds that he has had a genius of some sort all through their growing-up days. He might be an exceptional orator, have a flair for logical discussion, or be particularly brave, polite, or generous. The boy does not contest for the position, but rather is elected without his knowledge. As tokens of his election, his comrades will present him with a heifer and a black club that will belong to him alone. From the time of his election until they are circumcised, the boys will respect this one boy very highly. At times they will swear by using his name—as in "For Ng'atait's sake, I swear I didn't do that"—and such an oath is trustworthy, for no one may mock the leader's name. If the boys are satisfied with the elected boy, he will continue to be their leader even after they have been initiated into warriorhood, and all the way to elderhood. They may also replace him if they are dissatisfied. He must always participate in all meetings and ceremonies held in his locality and is regarded with all respect.

Soon after the *Alamal Lengipaata* ceremony is completed, circumcision starts, beginning with the older youths. The individual families of the youths have the final say on when their sons will be circumcised and, at this point, some families will rush to circumcise their youths while others will delay. Three or four years later, at the end of the circumcision period, the *Laibon* curses the knife used for the ceremony, saying, "Anyone who is circumcised after this point, may the knife kill him." The elder sponsors then break the *olpiron*, the symbolic stick used to kindle the ceremonial fire during circumcision. The circumcision period will not open again for approximately fifteen years, until the *Laibon* reblesses the knife and the elders repair the broken stick by binding it together.

Some sections of Maasailand, such as the Ilpurko, Iloitai, and most Kenyan Maasai, have what is called right-hand and left-hand circumcisions. As the time for circumcision approaches, all the eligible youths in these sections are divided into two groups according to age. The older group of boys, called the right-hand circumcision, is initiated first. They will remain warriors for seven years, at which point the younger boys, now grown, are ready to be circumcised. This newly initiated group will become the left-hand circumcision and take over from the right-hand warriors, who will graduate into junior elderhood. In five or six years, the left-hand circumcision group will graduate from warriorhood, and both groups will be united into one generation at *Olngesherr* ceremony, which is the confirmation of elderhood. (The Tanzanian Maasai have one continuous generation of warriors without a breakdown into right-hand and left-hand groupings.)

With circumcision a whole new life begins— new dress and ornamentation, new behavior, new activities, and above all a new freedom that the youths never had before as mere boys. They can now socialize with girls and have sex. They are free to roam Maasailand without asking their parents' permission. They have more control over their destiny and some degree of decision-making power. They can shake hands with other men as equals, instead of bending their heads to others in the respectful greeting of a child. And, most significantly, they attain the high degree of confidence that is known and enjoyed only by Maasai warriors after total manhood.

Childhood is a time of
great freedom for the Maasai. Until about the age of
seven, Maasai boys and girls have little to do in
the family group except play, learn the ways of the
adults, and build their language skills. Girls gradually
learn the womanly arts—making clothing, preparing
and maintaining household articles, milking the
animals, doing beadwork. Boys develop their
running and throwing skills, begin to learn about cattle,
and play at being herdsmen. Children of both sexes
are treated with the greatest tenderness and love,
not only by their parents but by most adults as well.
The self-confidence of adulthood is built
in these young years.

Maasai fathers spend a great deal of time with their children (*above, left*), tending even small babies with unusual care and concern. When not in the company of either parent, a Maasai child is likely to be looked after by an older sister. In Maasai society, however, children are never very far from adults and even if parents may be absent, elder men or women, whether related or not, will keep a close eye on the activities of the children in their settlement.

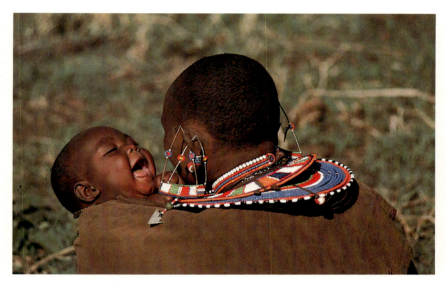

Maasai mothers and babies share a loving relationship, filled with physical contact and nurturing. Small babies are cuddled, tickled, nursed, and held; they are encouraged to explore their immediate world, which brings them into direct knowledge of the activities of Maasai life. As a mark of their treasured status among Maasai families, even the youngest children are adorned with bead necklaces and waistbands or wire bracelets and may be given special leather amulets to ward off misfortune.

Like children everywhere, Maasai youngsters imitate their elders in play, invent games, and simply test their physical abilities—running, jumping, throwing, tumbling, fighting. *Above, left*, three little ones play cattle herder, even using a makeshift herding stick. *To the right*, a boy shows two younger ones how to play the cattle game. Stones representing cows, bulls, and oxen are led into and out of a make-believe *engang,* a rough circle of dirt. *Below, left*, a file of girls plays "follow the leader" as a boy wields an oversized spear; *to the right*, older girls use rough pebbles to play the world-wide game of "jacks." *Opposite*, a thirsty tot drains his mother's calabash of the last drops of tasty milk.

As small boys learn to care for animals, girls learn the
womanly arts of Maasai life when they are strong
enough to assist in daily chores. *Opposite*, a girl works at
cleaning out an *olmosori*, a large calabash used in
brewing honey beer. She removes and squeezes out the
"sausage fruits" of the *Kigelia africana* tree, which are
put in the brew during the fermenting process.
Above, a girl lugs home a rolled-up mat, called *esos*, made
of long strands of lion grass woven together with leather
thongs. Such mats are used inside Maasai houses to
create pens for infant animals.

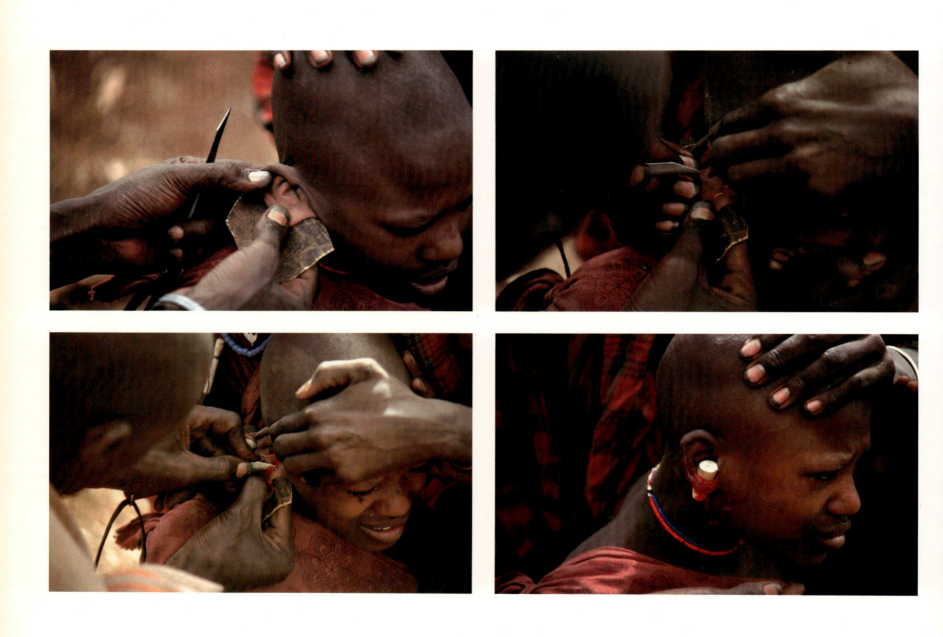

Adornment for beauty starts early among Maasai males and females alike. Ear piercing, usually done before circumcision and here performed on a girl, begins with an incision in the lobe of the ear; a small circle of flesh is removed and a short, freshly peeled section of green branch is inserted. Over many months, the opening is enlarged with wads of rolled leaves and a wooden plug. The lobe may then be decorated with beaded strands, leather flaps, buttons, silver and copper ornaments, and other trinkets. Ocher, a reddish mineral ground and mixed with animal fat, is the most widely used cosmetic. It is applied all over the body—even, at times, on the ears of girls.

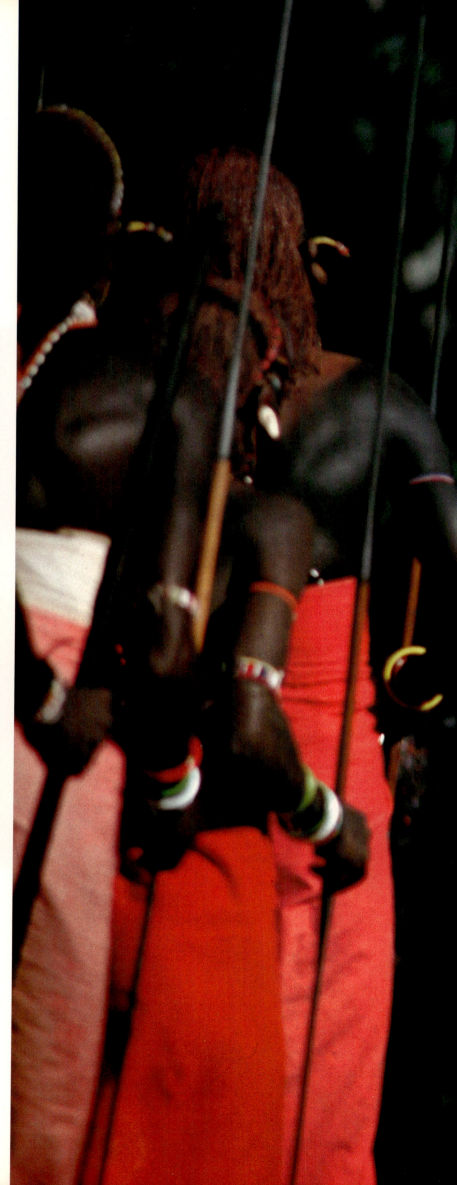

Above, a young woman with long flap earrings sings for the warrior she loves. *Opposite*, another woman dances with a group of warriors, some of them Samburu, a people closely related to the Maasai in language, dress, and custom.

Emorata: Circumcision

Emorata, or circumcision, the initiation of a boy or girl into adulthood, is for the Maasai a mental as well as a physical process. They believe that the youth who survives unflinchingly the pain of such an operation will emerge a man or woman able to endure the challenges of life. By the words of the circumcision ceremony, the youth is ordered to "wake up"— to leave behind childhood and assume adult responsibilities.

As we have seen, it is the dream of every Maasai boy to become a man one day and, if possible, as soon as he can. In case one's age-mate is circumcised first, all his other age-mates must grant him the respect adult males are given. The uninitiated boys find it extremely painful to do so, and cry bitterly to their parents to be initiated into manhood as well. For Maasai girls, however, initiation into womanhood is a totally different experience. They cannot believe that their beloved parents could do such a terrible thing to them. For to them circumcision will mean losing their freedom and going into strict married life. They will no longer enjoy the company of warriors nor can they choose their lovers as freely as before. Since men do not marry until they become junior elders (usually between the ages of twenty-six and thirty-five), the girls are likely to be married to men much older than themselves.

Girls are circumcised as soon as they reach puberty, or shortly thereafter. Unlike boys, they do not have generation-grouping, and so their circumcisions are individual depending on when their families decide to do them. If an uncircumcised girl becomes pregnant she is circumcised immediately, since in Maasailand children must not give birth to children. Grown-up girls are very careful not to have sex during their fertile period since pregnancy before circumcision is an extreme embarrassment to their families. In the past, certain *Laibon* families would abandon a daughter to the mercy of hyenas and jackals if they found her pregnant before circumcision.

Boys awaiting circumcision must follow certain procedures in preparation. The circumcision must be announced two months ahead of time to give the family ample time to prepare. There are articles that must be collected, such as ostrich feathers, honey, and wax, and a special bull must be found for the day of the ceremony. A house for the newly circumcised youth must be built, or the old house repaired and made warm and cozy. Such procedures may differ slightly from family to family, clan to clan, but in general they follow the same pattern. Some families, for instance, will hold the initiation at noon in the middle of the kraal instead of the more usual early morning ceremony by the main cattle entrance.

At left:
A newly circumcised boy wears his mother's
brass ornaments, blue ceremonial beads, and a stalk
of green grass symbolic of prosperity.

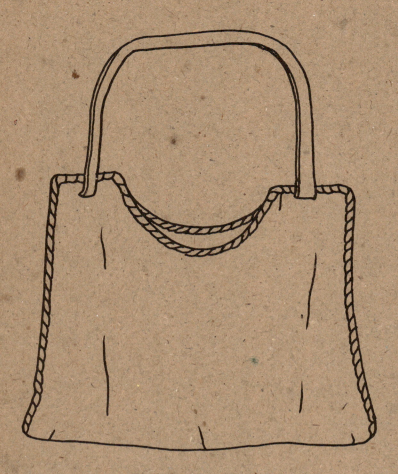

Hide container for honey beer

One shared custom is the procurement of honey. This was a difficult undertaking in the olden days, but today most people buy the honey from beekeepers such as the Ndorobo tribesmen or from outside traders. The honey is a most important part of the preparation since it is used to make the beer that must be drunk by the elders and guests at the ceremony. In the past, collecting honey was left to the boy by his parents, who felt that a boy wanting initiation must be ready to meet every challenge. The following story is told of such an instance:

A grown-up boy, ready and desperate to be made a complete man, had to go in search of honey. The bees had made their nest in a hollow on the side of a steep cliff, a difficult and dangerous spot to get at. The boy, therefore, fetched a long hide rope to help him descend the side of the cliff, which was so steep that if he loosened his grasp on the rope for even one moment it would be his end. He descended slowly and carefully. On his back he carried a hide bag to put the honey in, and in one hand he held a lit torch to smoke out the bees. He managed to reach the bees' nest and, without wasting any time, he smoked out the bees and collected the honey, which filled his hide bag to bursting. He started his ascent, climbing higher and higher. He had almost reached the top of the cliff when disaster struck. While the boy was climbing, a hyena had come along and had begun to chew the rope. With a cruel snap, the rope broke, throwing both the hyena and the boy into the canyon below. Both died instantly.

Fortunately, it is much easier today to procure honey. Once the honey is procured, the beer may take up to three weeks to prepare. The honey is mixed with water and certain roots. This liquid is then poured into a large, round calabash or into a specially made hide container and is placed near the fire. With constant tending, the beer ferments in two weeks, and in the third week it is filtered and divided among as many gourds as will be needed for the number of expected guests. One gourd is put aside for very special guests who are likely to bring presents of cattle to the family.

Another task facing the boy in the weeks prior to circumcision is the collecting of ostrich feathers and wax. After circumcision, the feathers will be used to start the youth's headdress, and the wax will be applied to the tips of his newly acquired arrows, which will become a prized possession, carried with him everywhere. The arrows are blunted with wax so that they will not hurt the young girls he playfully shoots at in an attempt to obtain their finger-rings.

Three days before the circumcision, a group of special elders, the *Loongoroki*, is formally called together to drink part of the honey beer, leaving the rest for the actual day of the ceremony. On the next day, the boy's head is shaved, and all his belongings are given away since he must not retain any ornament or possession of his youth when he becomes a man. On that day also he is anointed with ghee and dressed in a garment made of a special hide cloth resembling that worn by women.

The boy spends the day before the ceremony searching for a special African olive sapling called *alatim*. A symbol of his new manhood, this young tree will be planted the next day by the side of the house where he will stay after the operation. On this day, also, the boy has his first meeting with the circumciser, or *alamoratani*. This specialist, often a Ndorobo tribesman brought in from outside, will be paid one goat for each circumcision performed. At this first meeting the *alamoratani* hands the specially made circumcision knives to the boy, who will sharpen them himself and keep them safely until the following day. This precaution is taken because of the fear that some ill-intended person, who may wish to shame the family, may try to blunt the knives to inflict more pain on the boy. In some sections of Maasailand, it is believed that if a youth has secretly had sex with a circumcised woman, his circumcision knife will be cursed. He can lift the curse only by revealing his transgression on the day of the ceremony and by paying a cow to his family and to the circumciser. He must, however, undergo the operation without the customary help of someone to support his back.

During the entire day before the circumcision, the youths who have already been circumcised sing songs of encouragement to the expectant boy. Such songs are often crudely worded:

> *Etesheka alayoni kirora, negil engineji emowarak, negil osilalei otoiyo nedung elajang'ak engutukie. Neeku ilengolong joyoroo. Kanyoo naitengid kimola enjabin alayok tururi.*

> The boy farted while we were sleeping and the horrendous smell killed all the flies. The loud noise broke all the goats' horns as well as a dry tree. What makes him, with a foreskin penis, so proud?

These songs are meant to insult the boy and anger him so much that he will be better able to stand the pain of the knife. Some songs tell, in graphic terms, what will happen to the boy the following day if he

Calabash and "sausage fruits" used in making honey beer

"kicks the knife." The already circumcised youths taunt the boy by mimicking him and poking him on the neck and nostrils with arrows coated with a smelly wax. Some of the songs they sing, however, are meant to encourage the boy in a more gentle way:

Eiya ikiraposh engipa neiya isikitok endawo nimikinjoo
ilkasiod oowap engejek endungi.

Coward, the gray, colorless birds will be yours.
Brave man, the red-winged touracos will be yours,
and so will the green lovebirds.

The singing continues until it is time to sleep. As the others retire one by one, the candidate for circumcision often faces a sleepless night.

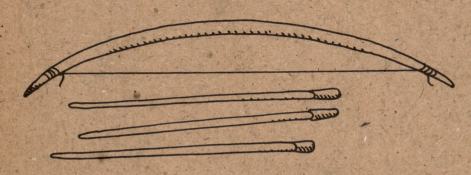

Bow and arrows of a newly circumcised youth

At early dawn of the next day, the boy is called out by the *ispolio*, the most recently circumcised youths, who sing to him once more. Tensely, his close relatives speak cruel words to him—"Go and shame us, youth" or "You'd better face it, it is blood that will flow, not milk." As the rising sun strikes the horns of the cattle, the boy is summoned to take his place by the main cattle gate. His mother gives him the hide of an unblemished ox, one that was slaughtered and did not die from disease, to sit on. The boy is stripped naked, and a close relative washes him from the head down with cold water. This water, called *engare endolu* (literally, "ax-water"), has been kept outside overnight with an ax-head placed inside the container to make it colder. This washing symbolically marks the boy's entrance into a whole new life by cleaning away all the wrongdoing he has committed during his past life as a youth. On a more practical level, it also numbs him somewhat for the operation.

An elder has already been selected to hold the boy's back. He must be a close relative who is trusted enough to support the boy. There is a story told in Maasailand that once the supporter of a boy drove a long prickly thorn into the boy's back to make him flinch so as to disrupt the ceremony and disgrace the boy. In that case, the brave boy did not react until it was all over and then accused the wrongdoer, who was most severely reprimanded.

As soon as the boy is washed, he walks to the place of circumcision, which is usually in the center of the kraal or on the right side of his father's entrance to the kraal, and sits down on a hide placed there. The back supporter is already there, and soon the circumciser appears and waits for the boy to sit facing him with his legs wide open. The boy has already been advised concerning how to behave during the operation. For instance, once he has assumed a position facing a certain direction, he will have to maintain it until the operation is over. Also, since the time he was young, he has practiced how to control blinking by telling his friends to pinch him hard while he steadied his eyes. If he succeeds in controlling his blinking, it is believed he will also succeed in not flinching during the operation. Once the boy is set, the circumciser splashes his face with *enturoto*, a chalky white mineral mixed with water or milk which is often used in Maasai ceremonies as a symbolic blessing.

As the *enturoto* strikes the boy's face, the circumciser announces, "One cut." This is a formal pronouncement uttered so as not to take the boy by surprise, because soon after the announcement there follows a sharp knife through the boy's foreskin. Gathered around the boy are males of all ages, residents of the kraal and visitors, who have come to witness both the operation and the boy's performance. Only males are permitted to watch a boy's circumcision, and only females are allowed to witness a girl's. The operation takes about five minutes, after which the circumciser calls for milk to wash the boy and the knife. This milk must be from an unblemished cow, one whose calves are all living. It is placed in a special gourd or calabash and given, with some green grass, to the circumciser, who will wash the boy with it.

With the call to bring milk, the immense tension that has prevailed for two days and taken its toll during the operation subsides, and people begin to relax. One hears cries of praise from the boy's immediate relatives, particularly his mother, who has been collecting the milk for washing her son after the operation and has probably been thinking of hiding to avoid being beaten if the boy has been a coward. They will say things like "I knew he would make it through." Others with a sense of humor will sometimes say, "He is too ugly to be a coward." The Maasai believe that one cannot be both ugly and a coward since God would not be so cruel as to give one person two bad things.

Once he has been washed with the milk, the boy is ordered, "Wake up, you are now a man." In some families, the boy will remain seated to wait for his relatives, the admirers of his bravery, to give him cattle as presents. When it is announced that the boy has refused to wake up, the relatives will come up to him one by one and say, "Wake up, so I can give you this or that animal." When the boy thinks he has been given enough cattle to reward his patience and courage he will stand up. Assisted by his back supporter, he is slowly led to his mother's house, where he will rest and nurse his wound.

In the case of a boy who has cried out during the operation, the spectators will declare him a coward and will not partake of the meat, milk, or honey beer provided by his parents for the occasion. A ceremony that has taken a month or more to prepare will be useless. The youth is termed one who has "kicked the knife," and along with his family he will be disgraced. His father and mother will be spat upon for having raised a coward. The family's cattle within the kraal will be beaten until they stampede and break through the fence. The boy will also receive a thorough beating. The food he eats will be spat upon and he must eat all of it. Although this bitter embarrassment will follow him for some time, people will eventually forget it and accept him again.

The procedure for female circumcision is in many ways similar to that for the male. Wax and ostrich feathers are not required, and the parents of the girl rather than the girl herself must search for the honey. The girl's head is shaved like the boy's and she also gives away all of her old ornaments and clothing. The day before the ceremony, the *alatim* sapling is collected to be planted beside her house.

The female circumcision, or clitoridectomy, involves the removal of the clitoris and labia minora. A specialist, who must be a woman, is brought in from the outside to perform the operation. She uses a specially made, curved and highly sharpened piece of metal. The girl is circumcised inside her mother's house, the light for the operation coming from a hole in the roof particularly cut for that purpose. Extremes of courage are not demanded of the girls, and they are not sung to by their peers to induce courage. Although they must go through initiation, they are not punished if they cry out as long as they allow the operation to continue. The really timid girls, who may try to get loose during the circumcision, are held down by the women present; if this fails, warriors will be summoned to help in holding them down. If a girl goes through the operation unflinchingly she is sometimes teasingly told to yell *Uui* so as not to equal the courage of boys, but in most cases she will refuse. Girls who undergo the operation are usually given cattle, perhaps she-lambs, heifers, or even milk cows, by those relatives present, but only if they feel like honoring the girl. At the end of the circumcision day the girl, covered by a beaded hide, is led out of the house by the women and the circumciser to be examined.

There is much activity and celebration after the successfully circumcised boy or girl is led away to recuperate. The warriors are in charge of slaughtering an ox for the feast. Others obtain a cow's blood, which will be mixed with sour milk to make a drink called *asaroi*, the first food the newly circumcised youth takes.

Well-dressed and beautifully decorated warriors and women pour in from kraals both near and far to join in the celebration. A group of singing warriors and girls carry the *alatim* tree to the side of the house where the boy or girl is resting, and several women plant it there as they sing the praises of the newly circumcised. Those women who know the relatives personally bring them gifts of calabashes filled with milk. Everyone present feasts and dances as the elders continue to drink the honey beer they started two days before.

During their healing periods, both the newly circumcised boy and girl are very well fed and carefully nursed. They are given melted animal fat to drink, for the Maasai believe it will help them to heal faster. For several days after the ceremony, the other newly circumcised youths stay with the boy to keep him company, share his food, and talk with him. They help him in preparing his headdress made of ostrich feathers and stuffed birds and in making his arrows and blunting them with wax. While the young circumcised girls go through a similar period of healing after their operation, they do not congregate like the boys. They dress in black beaded hides and wear a circular band around their heads, with long, loose links of metal chain or beads hanging down over their eyes. The girls are not allowed to be seen or talked to by strangers, particularly men. When they have healed, they will prepare for married life.

When the newly circumcised boy heals enough to be able to walk, his comrades decorate him with white facepaint and then lead him outside. The boy spends his time playfully shooting at young girls with his arrows and hunting birds for his headdress. If he has withstood the operation unflinchingly, he may kill colorful birds such as touracos, lovebirds, Diana's barbets, and sunbirds, but if he has cried out, he may use only unattractive gray ones such as cisticola birds. Soon the boy and his comrades begin a journey that will take them all over Maasailand to visit other kraals in which circumcisions are taking place.

Wherever they go in Maasailand, they are fed and treated well by everyone so they can regain their strength. They are not allowed to wash during this period of healing for fear of catching cold, nor are they allowed to touch food with their bare hands because they are considered unclean. Instead, they use specially made sharp sticks to eat their meat, which is cut into small pieces. Newly circumcised boys are very conspicuous—they wear either animal hides blackened with charcoal and oil or black garments also smeared with oil. Attached to their headdresses or worn at their temples are *isurutia*, the round, coiled ornaments made of brass usually worn by women. A boy in this state is considered to be similar to a woman who has just given birth, weak and needing to be taken care of.

The newly circumcised youths continue to roam freely, singing to the boys preparing for circumcision and encouraging them as they themselves were encouraged. They remain in this state for two to three months, until they are fully healed. They wear black all this time and let their hair grow. They are not shaved until they have finished making their crown headdress of beautiful stuffed birds. After the birds are caught, their insides are removed and stuffed with grass to prevent odor. The stuffed birds are then attached to a circular frame and form a crownlike shape. These headdresses are important to the warriors since they are used for ceremonies and dances. When their crowns are completely filled with birds, the young men are shaved for the last time until elderhood. Some sections then perform a transitional ceremony, called *Embolosata Olkiteng*, in which the young men are blessed in several different ways by their elder sponsors. And then they move into a different stage of life.

They become young warriors. They let their hair grow long and spend much time in grooming it. Everything they wear must be new to symbolize a new life. They remove their stuffed bird headdresses and their old clothing with all its accumulated black color and replace them with the warrior's distinctive hair style and togas dyed with red ocher. They also cover their bodies from head to toe with the same red ocher. Their parents give the warriors new long spears, and their mothers and girl friends make all new beaded ornaments for them. With all these new colors, clothes, necklaces, and earrings, the circumcised youths emerge into total warriorhood.

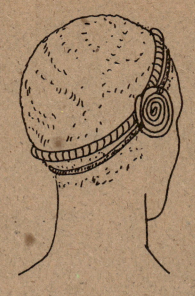

The coiled brass ornaments (isurutia) *and headband of blue beads* (engonongoi) *worn by the new warrior*

Circumcision marks the initiation
of adolescent boys and girls into adulthood
and serves as a kind of proof that they are prepared to
endure the challenges of life with courage and dignity.
Following circumcision, males become warriors; females
enter married life. Circumcision takes place at dawn.
A boy undergoes circumcision just outside the main
cattle gate of his family enclosure; a girl is initiated
inside her mother's house. Following the rite, the
father of the newly circumcised youth blesses his
cattle in a special way, spraying them with milk and
honey beer from a calabash lightly stuffed with fresh
grass as a symbol of prosperity. A young sapling is
planted next to the initiate's house to
signify the important passage.

Using an arrow wrapped with a thong just behind its tip so that it does not penetrate too deeply, a warrior shoots carefully into the jugular vein of a heifer to draw off blood that will be given to a newly circumcised boy or girl. Caught in a calabash, the blood is mixed with sour milk and forms the first food given to the new initiate. The animal's wound is sealed with a bit of dung, and it is released relatively unharmed after the ritual bloodletting.

Dressed in charcoal-darkened cloth, generation-mates of the new initiate gather to celebrate in song and dance.

Newly circumcised warriors shoot at girls with blunted arrows
to win their beaded finger-rings.

During the last months of their healing after a successful, unflinching circumcision, and before their confirmation as warriors, the young men prepare colorful bird headdresses for themselves. Roaming widely, they hunt and kill such birds as kingfishers, orioles, and bee-eaters *(pictured above)* as well as Diana's barbets and lovebirds. Each bird that is brought down is cleaned, stuffed with ashes and dried grass, and then attached to a large, horseshoe-shaped crown. It may take up to forty birds to complete such a headdress. Throughout his period of healing, the headdress is a prized possession of the young man, worn by him at ceremonies and dances.

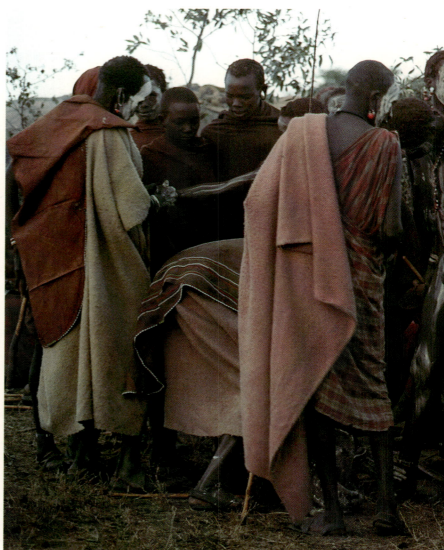

As a final confirmation of their newly acquired warrior status, the youths of some sections undergo a ceremony called *Embolosata Olkiteng*. First, the mothers of the young men build a ceremonial manyatta, an enclosure consisting of forty-nine hide-covered shelters. Within the manyatta they build another, smaller circle made of lion-grass mats. Here, the ritual events take place, sometimes with as many as 700 youths participating.

Among various blessings given over several days by a group of elder sponsors is a ritual daubing with white pigment called *enturoto*. The elders first apply *enturoto* to one another, and then they streak each young man's face

and body with white. *Following pages*, a ceremonial ox is slaughtered and the elders move around a circle of seated youths, smearing their foreheads with fatty meat and offering each a bite. Finger-rings fashioned from strips of the ox's stomach skin are placed on the middle fingers of all the new warriors. Then, seated in a mass inside the ritual circle and ringed with bunches of fresh grass brought in by the elders, the warriors are showered with honey beer spat upon them by the elders. At the end of the ceremony, the warriors circle the enclosure, singing, and file out on their way to new lives, blessed by the elders.

Ilmoran: Warriors

*Ilbarnot, Ilbarnot naa—ingiri naapir ishoree—pemeisho
lelo engishu ilmang'ati nemeisho si engilome alamei eibok
si enkinyala naepu engujit elikai supuko.*

Young are the warriors, and we feed them the
best of our meat. Healthy, they will protect our
herds from enemies and famine. And they will
stop all the foes of our people from encroaching
upon us.

These words, sung by senior warriors to their younger
comrades during their feasting camps, express
something of the significance and the almost magical
powers attributed to the title *ilmoran* ("warriors") in
Maasailand. Whenever there is work requiring
strength or courage people will ask, "Are there no
warriors around today?" Warriors are needed both for
simple tasks—capturing a cow to be slaughtered for a
ceremony and decorating it with bells, wrestling with
one to be branded—and for dangerous ones—
protecting the herd from lions or subduing a crazy
rhino charging through the kraal. Maasai warriors in
their prime seldom fall short in the performance of
their duties. When praised, they will modestly answer,
"All we did is what Maasai warriors are supposed to do."

I remember from my own experience as a warrior
how self-confidence takes over the whole being, along
with pride and a feeling of ease, as if you yourself and
all those around you were thinking, "Everything will be
all right as long as the warriors are here." We were
supposed to be brave, brilliant, great lovers, fearless,
athletic, arrogant, wise, and above all concerned
with the well-being of our comrades and of the Maasai
community as a whole. We realized that we were totally
trusted by our community for protection, and we tried to
live up to their expectations. If, for example, a lion
would roar near our kraal at night, we would be so
insulted at his boldness. All we would wish for was
daybreak so that we might go in search of him, hunt
him, and teach him a lesson: that we warriors, and not
he, reign supreme. We used to say that until a lion could
roast his meat, that is, stop eating raw meat, he would
never be able to challenge us. And we used to boast
that, although a lion could run faster than we could, we
could run farther.

Maasai warriors are so fearless that a German
writer by the name of Karl Peters observed, at the turn
of the century, "The only thing that would make an
impression on these wild sons of the steppe was a
bullet... and then only when employed in emphatic
relation to their own bodies." Warriors are reputed to
be afraid of nothing short of Almighty God; even
foreigners do not scare them. Often they do not bother
to distinguish persons dressed in foreign clothes from

*At left:
A Maasai warrior in full regalia, with his buffalo-hide
shield, carries a fragrant bunch of leleshwa leaves
beneath his arm as a deodorant.*

Warrior hairstyle and neckbands

each other, be they white or black. They sum up foreigners with the word *ilmeek*, meaning "aliens," or *iloridaa enjekat*, meaning "those who confine their farts." This last term refers to the nature of European clothes, which do not allow the wind to blow away any unwanted odors, as does the Maasai toga.

The arrogance of warriors is so obvious at times. While they generally respect elders and respond to their wishes, they can defy their dictates if they find them improper. There is a known case of a warrior slashing off his earlobe and handing it to an elder who had the presumption to demand attention by saying, *Enjoki ingiyaa inyi*, "Lend me your ear." There are many legendary tales propounding the bravery and arrogance of warriorhood. During the days when there was much fighting between different sections of Maasai, one such incident occurred:

An Ilkisongo warrior from Tanzania was resting his head on a lion he had just killed when, out of the bush, an enemy contingent appeared and saw him lying there. Completely unconcerned, the warrior did not express any fear whatsoever. Several of the enemy contingent raised their spears and charged toward him, meaning to kill him, but they were stopped by their leader, who realized and appreciated the daredevil behavior of the unbudging warrior. The Ilkisongo warrior, however, had no intention of thanking the one who saved his life. Instead, he lifted his head and angrily told the man who saved him, "Curse you, I didn't ask for that favor! Why didn't you let your warriors finish their job? Don't ever do that again—I am not your kith and kin."

Besides this most important quality of bravery, Maasai warriors have many other virtues. One of these is the strong comradeship they feel for each other. Maasai warriors share practically everything, from food to women. According to tradition, a warrior must never eat alone. This was first made a law in order to ensure that every warrior, even one from the poorest family, would have enough to eat. And, even today, warriors roam Maasailand always in groups, never alone, for this reason. There are even certain sections that forbid a warrior to drink milk from his own cattle, in an attempt to encourage sharing rather than selfish monopoly.

Visitors to Maasailand have commented on the cordiality, intelligence, and honesty they found there. Edgar M. Queeny, in a *National Geographic* expedition through Maasailand in 1954, wrote that the cooperation he received from the Maasai warriors "varied only in the degree of excellence. Their good humour never failed. They anticipated our wants beyond any reasonable expectation, and their manner and natural impulses were those which, in our own society, we would attribute to gentlemen." And Sidney Hinde, Britain's first resident among these warrior tribesmen, observed in his book *The Last of the Maasai* (1910), "The Maasai are quick at learning. As a race they are intelligent and truthful, and a grown Maasai will neither thieve nor lie. He may refuse to answer a question but, once given, his word can be depended on."

Finally, warriors bring excitement, adventure, and romance to the kraal. In their songs and dances, they celebrate legendary cattle raids, brave men, or simply life in general. They hunt dangerous animals in order to defend their herds or to obtain skins and manes to decorate their bodies—and, sometimes, just for the pleasure of it. In their prime, warriors are very active sexually and frequently capture women's hearts. One will always see girls giggling whenever warriors are around. The warriors will pretend not to notice but, in truth, they are fully aware. They will spend much time singing with these young uncircumcised girls at night and sometimes in the daytime as well. Life in the kraal is seldom lonely when warriors are near.

The physical appearance of the Maasai warrior expresses all the qualities that the Maasai, and even many foreigners, consider desirable. This is particularly true when the warriors are seen in full war gear on their way to a cattle raid or to retrieve stolen cattle. Like finely crafted bronze statues, the warriors appear in full regalia with headdresses of gleaming black ostrich feathers or lions' manes, elaborately patterned shields of buffalo hides, and spears glistening in the sun. They are both admirable and awe-inspiring. The early explorers of Maasailand often noted the impressive costume and bearing of the warriors. In *Through Masai Land*, Joseph Thomson had this to say: "We soon set our eyes upon the dreaded warriors that had been so long the subject of my waking dreams, and I could not but involuntarily exclaim 'What splendid fellows!' as I surveyed a band of the most peculiar race of men to be found in Africa." Although one may be opposed to the raids and the battles for which the warriors put on this impressive dress, one cannot help but admire its beauty. Peter Matthiessen, in his book *The Tree Where Man Was Born* (1974), wrote that Myles, his white companion born and bred in East Africa, "much regrets the passing of the days when stately files of Maasai raiders in black ostrich plumes and lions' headdress, spear points gleaming, crossed the plains without a sideways glance." Today, restricted by the ban on hunting wild animals, the

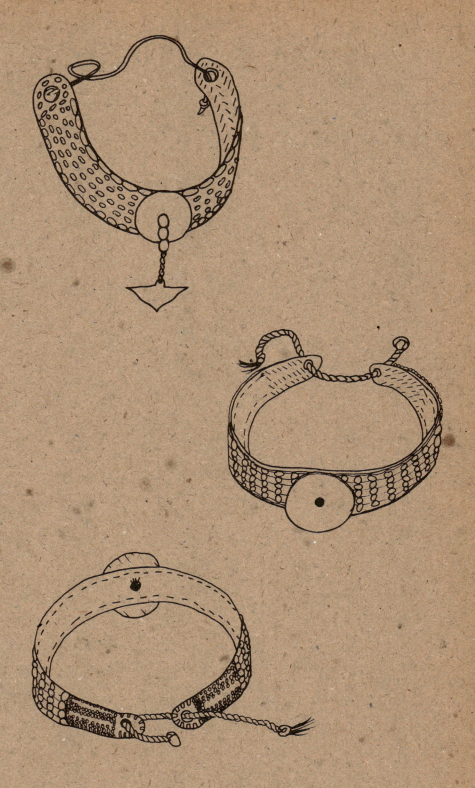

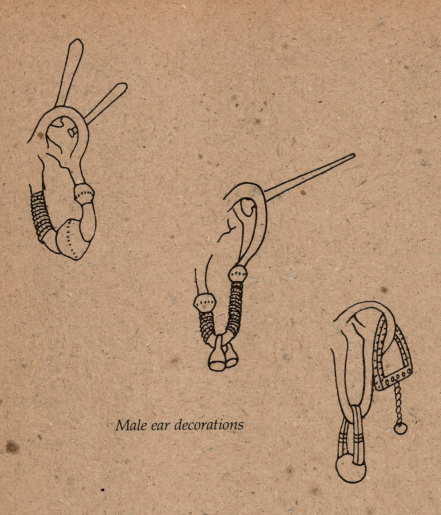

Male ear decorations

Maasai find it harder and harder to obtain buffalo hides for their shields and lions' manes for their headdresses.

Their physical beauty and the decoration of their bodies are important to Maasai warriors in times of peace as well. Anxious to attract girls, they spend hours decorating themselves with ocher and plaiting their hair. They first grind the ocher, then mix it with fat or water. After this mixture is applied to the legs and while it is still wet, decorative patterns are drawn with the fingertips or a stick. Warriors braid their hair into long plaits, often twisting in strands of wool to create greater length, and then dye it red with a mixture of ocher and fat. They adorn their earlobes, necks, arms, waists, and ankles with the beaded ornaments made by their female suitors.

When a girl decides to formally declare her love for a warrior, she invites him to her house to drink milk. The girl will make a formal announcement to her parents that she loves a particular warrior, and her mother will then prepare a large quantity of milk to be drunk on the day selected for the warrior and his friends to come by. On that day, contingents of warriors celebrate and sing, going from one kraal to another, drinking milk with their girl friends and feasting merrily.

Maasai girls usually select three lovers from among the warriors. The first is *asanja* ("the sweetheart") and is the one for whom she prepares the milk. The second one is *oljipet* ("the skewer"), who takes over when the first is not present, as does the third, *olkeloki* ("the one who crosses over"), when the first and second are not near. There is no jealousy among the three lovers, but they must respect each other's status in relation to the girl. The girl may still sleep with other warriors, but she may do so only if none of her three formal lovers is present. The girl will continue seeing these lovers until her marriage.

The ever-present spear of a Maasai warrior is a most precious possession. A traveler in Maasailand often sees the lightning flash of a Maasai spearpoint gleaming in the distance before the silhouetted body of a warrior appears. The warriors develop a worshipful trust in their weapons, and certain braves will never flee from an attack as long as their spears are still in their hands, for fleeing would be like betraying their weapons. The warrior anoints his spear with animal fat and polishes it often to prevent rusting. All day long, the spear is held in the warrior's hand or thrust, point up, into the ground by his side. It would be considered a serious insult to a Maasai warrior if anyone were to insert his spearpoint into the ground. At night it is stored inside by his girl friends. Not used for fighting alone, the spears are sometimes decorated to symbolize peace. Pure black ostrich feathers are attached to the tip of the spear with a string of beads, forming a round crown. A piece of black ebony may be inserted into the spear shaft to indicate a warrior's seniority, while a section of pale wood indicates his junior status.

Young Maasai men properly initiated into warriorhood first become *ilkeliani*, or junior warriors. In order to increase their strength and bravery these junior warriors participate, with senior warriors, in special feasting camps called *olpul*. The first feasting camp they go to as young warriors is called *olkiteng loo ngulalen* ("the bull to insert ear plugs"). This name derives from the fact that the new warrior must wear wooden plugs inserted in the holes of his ears until the end of this camp. While in the camp, the warriors must also remove all their ornaments and ocher make-up. For their entire stay in the camp, often as long as a month or so, the warriors are prohibited from having sexual relations, either with the uncircumcised girls at the camp or with the circumcised women they meet when they go to the village to obtain oxen for slaughter.

The feasting camp is made ready in the following way. About six to ten warriors meet to select several fine bullocks for slaughter. If an individual does not have his own bullock, he may exchange a heifer or a couple of three-year-old calves for one fine bull. When all of the necessary bullocks are found, the warriors collect cooking materials such as pots and knives. They go out a long distance from their homes, exploring the territory to find a suitable place to build their camp. It must be a secluded place by a sweet stream away from any intrusion. After the warriors find a good spot—a large cave or a clearing in a forest—they return home to prepare for the slaughtering day.

The day of the slaughtering is the busiest of all. Two strong warriors lead one of the selected bulls, on a strong rope, from their home kraal to the slaughtering camp. (A new bull will be brought each time the meat of the preceding one has been eaten.) This is a very difficult undertaking, since the bull, not wanting to leave the rest of the herd, will fight and struggle to get loose, but the warriors must not let him go. The site of the feasting camp is sometimes a long distance from home, and on the way, there will be places in which a bullock can hide and there may even be dangerous wild animals. The warriors who lead the bullock must therefore be trustworthy. The rest of the warriors will bring the cooking utensils and perhaps will take along some boys and girls also, believing that they will grow fast from eating meat. Children can also be helpful in doing chores such as collecting firewood and boiling soup. Circumcised women, however, are

A Maasai warrior with many of his ornaments

Warriors' patterned buffalo shields

never permitted in the camps since it is forbidden for warriors to eat meat in front of them.

The warriors slaughter each of the bulls brought to the camp, one at a time, and roast and boil the meat. They also make a soup by mixing the meat, special tree barks, and herbs, and they drink it for good digestion, strength, and courage. As they stay together in seclusion, a strong bond of comradeship develops among the warriors. The senior warriors teach the junior warriors in many *olpul* activities, instructing them in war tactics and planning cattle raids with them. The warriors spend their time exploring their surroundings and sometimes going out on hunts. When they kill a buffalo, they take the hide back to camp to make shields, which they decorate colorfully and paint with special marks to indicate bravery. These shields are a source of pride to their bearers as well as protection during wartime.

Despite the comradeship of the feasting camps, there is some rivalry felt between the two groups of warriors. For one thing, the girl friends of the senior warriors always show interest in a new group of young warriors. The senior warriors, finding it hard to accept their girl friends' deserting them for a new generation, will many times punish the new warriors by beating them. This often continues until all the youths of the new generation have been circumcised and increase in numbers and strength enough to defend themselves. Then, too, the senior warriors make much of the younger men's inexperience and set high standards of manhood and bravery for them to meet. Often mistreated and mocked by the older men, the new warriors will try to prove themselves by going on frequent lion hunts. The older warriors, not wanting to give them credit, scrutinize their skills in these hunts and harshly criticize them. If a junior warrior gets wounded during a hunt, the older warriors make a big issue out of it with such comments as, "What did I tell you? Such boys go on lion hunts only to offer themselves to lions, not to kill them." Even in feasting camps, the senior warriors will taunt the younger, saying things like *Meel ilbarnot engene.* Literally, this means, "Junior warriors will not even oil the rope" (the rope used to tie the bull while driving it to camp). The rope is oiled, as a gesture of gratitude, before returning it to the owner, and the expression implies that junior warriors are inexperienced and therefore untrustworthy.

As this competition between the younger and older warriors intensifies and the junior warriors increase in numbers, strength, and arrogance, the senior warriors are no longer able to withstand their force. The older warriors give over their control to the junior warriors and start to prepare themselves for elderhood. (This is the time when the young warriors are allowed to insert a section of black ebony into their spears.) Those junior warriors initiated in the first and second years of the recent circumcision period become the senior warriors, while those initiated in the third and fourth years take the place of the junior warriors. Once again there is friction, but it is not as intense because the junior and senior warriors now belong to one generation, having all been initiated during the same four-year period. They will remain warriors for a period of about fifteen years, from approximately their mid teens to their early thirties.

As new initiates, the junior Maasai warriors live with the rest of their families in kraals, but when they reach full maturity they go to live in a manyatta. This is a specially built kraal reserved for warriors, their trusted mothers, their girl friends not yet initiated, and several junior elder sponsors, the "fire-stick elders," who will instruct the warriors in Maasai customs. A manyatta brings together both junior and senior warriors and forms them into one unified body, breaking down any divisions existing between them. Although the warriors visit their parents' homes regularly and help in day-to-day activities, they take turns in doing this because their manyatta must never be unprotected.

Only those persons mentioned previously are allowed in the manyatta. Even uncircumcised youths, who would usually help the warriors in tending cattle, are not wanted. A beautiful site is chosen for the manyatta, one with access to water and good grazing. Forty-nine houses (a lucky number in Maasailand) are built there by the warriors' mothers, while the warriors themselves build the sprawling fence around the manyatta. The houses are made sturdy and spacious enough to accommodate the many warriors and their girl friends. In each house, the mother will build a private bed for herself and another bed for the warriors and their girl friends.

Everything in the manyatta must be the exclusive property of the warriors and the elders instructing them. Sufficient cattle for the manyatta can be difficult to obtain. If, for example, the parents of the warrior have only a few cattle, dividing these to send some to the manyatta will leave less milk for the family, and the family will therefore be reluctant to give up cattle for this purpose. There can even be difficulty in procuring the people necessary to form the manyatta. If the father of a warrior has married only one wife, he will find it hard to let his wife go to the warriors' manyatta, because he will have no one left to take care of him and his children.

Before the manyatta is built, certain warriors,

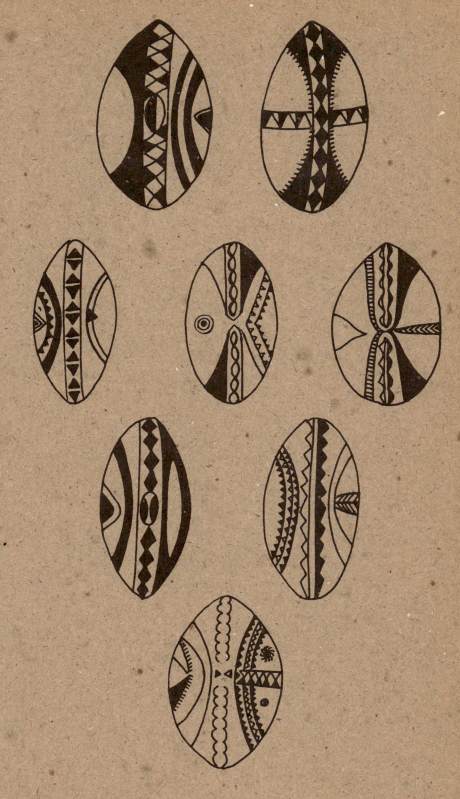

called the *embikas*, are selected by the warriors for their bravery and maturity. Usually dressed in full war regalia, this delegated group sweeps the country to obtain whatever is required for the manyatta, using force to obtain whatever they want. This group also has the responsibility of punishing or removing any unwanted elements within the warrior generation. These might include warriors who shave their long hair before graduation into elderhood or those who have refused to obey the elders and to pay the fine for their disobedience.

The *embikas* also act as a press-gang for recruiting those warriors who feel they have a more demanding responsibility to stay and help with the running of their family homes than to go to the manyatta. Unless a warrior's reasons are convincing, the delegation will force him and his cattle to come with them. If any warrior's mother or her husband is unwilling that she enter the manyatta, the delegation of warriors will weigh the objections and decide if she should be brought there. If the cattle needed for milk in the manyattas are not donated by the warriors' families, the *embikas* will take them by force. They may also impound the cattle of any wrongdoer, such as a warrior caught drinking milk without a companion. They may punish him by slaughtering some of his cattle and feasting on the meat or by taking some of his cattle as a gift to a *Laibon* who is to officiate over some warrior ceremony. In general, their duty is to ensure, by whatever means necessary, that the generation of warriors remains unblemished and of good repute.

Soon after construction of the manyatta has been completed, a procession of well-dressed warriors, with their mothers and girl friends, moves in to stay. The warriors interact very intensely and closely within the manyatta and learn much from the experience. For one thing, how they are regarded by others becomes clear. Reputations are made within the generation—one warrior may be regarded as brave, another as generous and kind, a third as cruel. Those with leadership qualities emerge and are recognized and consulted whenever there are important decisions to be made. A strong sense of clanship also develops, for the layout of the manyatta separates the Black Cow clan from the Red Cow clan.

The elders present in the manyatta act as ceremonial sponsors and instruct the warriors in the customs and values of Maasai society. With their advice and that of the *Laibon*, warriors learn to make and carry out their own decisions, such as when and how to raid cattle from neighboring peoples. The process of planning and organizing raids, carrying them out, and dividing the booty further strengthens the ties between members of a warrior generation.

Being in a manyatta makes most warriors more alert, proud, and competitive. They become anxious to show the warriors in other manyattas that they are the most courageous by staging many cattle raids and formal lion hunts. To discourage these forbidden activities, the governmental authorities in Maasailand, and particularly those in Kenya, have tried to shorten and regulate the time warriors spend in the manyattas. Certain manyattas, such as *Emanyatta e Kirtalo* in Loita and *Emanyatta Olorien* in the Ngorongoro Highlands, have become legendary because of the prowess of their warriors. These two manyattas, built during the warrior generation lasting from 1954 to 1975, were known all over Maasailand for the special courage of their warriors.

The activities of Maasai warriors are many. Within their family communities, they are very helpful, performing such tasks as building thorn fences to protect the herds, clearing sand from wells, and watering cattle during the harsh dry season. Warriors tend cattle only if they have no younger brothers to help them. When not working, the warriors group together to sing or play. A common game involves throwing wild sisal stalks or the round yellow fruits known as "Sodom apples" at each other and fending off the blows with their shields. This game gives them much practice in using their shields effectively. Sometimes they chase their beautiful girl friends, teasing them with branches, or get into mock fights with them.

Another activity of the warrior is called *enkitoongiwong*. This involves a vigilant exploration of their surroundings to obtain news and defend against danger. During feasting camps, warriors often enjoy such explorations armed with swords alone. *Enkitoongiwong* is a valued activity among the Maasai, depicted in many legends, like the following:

A young warrior happened to be exploring his surroundings while away from his slaughtering camp. He spotted two scouts who had been sent out from his camp to locate any enemy herds of cattle which might be raided later, when the days at slaughtering camp were over. Making sure not to be seen by the scouts, he followed them, knowing all along that he would not be allowed by the older warriors to be part of the cattle raids. He was still regarded as young and inexperienced, and had not even been allowed to attend the meeting to discuss the intended raid.

For two days he followed the scouts from

afar. On the third day, the scouts saw smoke and
dust but did not bother to go close enough to see
what was causing them. The scouts were sure that
the dust was stirred up by cattle and that the
smoke was a sign of people present. With only
those two signs of habitation, they returned to the
feasting camp and told their comrades how
successful they had been. They then sat and
waited for the end of the feasting camp so they
could lead their comrades on to a raid. The young
warrior, however, was dissatisfied and did not
return. He crept closer to the smoke and dust to
find out exactly where they came from, only to
discover that the dust was caused by stampeding
wildebeests coming to a river for water, and the
smoke by Ndorobo honey collectors smoking out
bees and cooking food.

After this discovery, the young warrior
decided to go ahead and try to fulfill the scouts'
role, to search for the cattle. He walked steadily
for one and a half days before he found a suitable
source of cattle. Wanting to be certain and not
repeat his comrades' mistake, he went very close
to the kraals of the enemy. In one kraal, he saw
and heard a woman calling to one of her cows.
The cow's name was Songori and it was white and
had a red calf, which it was nursing. After
learning the size of the herds in the surrounding
villages and when and how best to attack, the
young warrior went back to his camp satisfied.

He did not reveal his findings until the day
came for all the warriors to depart from the
slaughtering camp. Now, it is customary that
before departing the warriors must sing to the
heavens and the forest and to anyone present,
including the creatures of the forest, as a gesture
of thanks and gratitude for the peace they have
enjoyed and also as a farewell to the solitude. This
singing, called *enkipolosa*, takes place several times:
in the feasting camp on the evening preceding
departure; at early dawn of the next day; again in
the evening as the warriors leave camp; and as the
warriors are nearing home, to let their people
know of their return. Only warriors with beautiful
singing voices are selected for this task. Those
chosen try to take the warriors unawares when
they start to sing. Suddenly, their song will
shatter the peace, moaningly, as they sing out at
the top of their voices. The words of the song are
pure poetry, wise and reasonable. Such words
induce emotion in any human being, and people
are moved to tears.

In this particular feasting camp, the young
warrior who had spied on the scouts was the first

to sing. He stood in the singing place, which is usually the highest point overlooking the camp, to say goodbye to the forest and the murmur of waters. In a beautifully pitched voice he sang the following words, "Don't be fooled by stampeding wildebeestes. Don't be cheated by smoke caused by Ndorobo honey collectors. I peered and smiled at Songori and her calf. She is white with long horns and a red calf suckling. Come this way, those of you who want cattle."

The entire slaughtering camp was taken by surprise. The two warriors who had been the official scouts were flabbergasted and refused to accept the young warrior's words. The warriors were divided: some trusted the young warrior and followed him, others did not believe him and went with the warrior-scouts. The young warrior's vigilance and honesty, however, were rewarded in the end. Those who followed him were most successful in gaining cattle, while the others failed. And the young warrior took as his own, in addition to other cattle, the white cow named Songori and her red calf.

Although the government has forbidden them, cattle raids and lion hunts are still held, on a small scale, by Maasai warriors. Maasailand is so immense that it is hard for the government to patrol it properly. Before it was forbidden by the colonial governments in the early 1900s, cattle raiding was a popular and useful warrior's occupation. First, scouts would be sent out to find large non-Maasai herds suitable for raiding. They would return with cattle dung as proof of their success, and the necessary number of warriors, sometimes as many as one thousand, would be mobilized. After a ceremony in which they were formally blessed by the elders and were given a charm by a famous Laibon, the warriors would leave for the chosen destination. In recent days, cattle raiding is no longer a formal, colorful public display, but is instead pure theft. Those few diehard warriors who still raid must be very discreet, for if they were arrested by the government authorities they would be severely punished.

Because of their sacred love of cattle, however, the Maasai will always be enemies of any outsider, African or European, who keeps cattle. The warriors are still a Maasai standing army ready to defend their land and cattle from enemy attack. Tall, handsome, and fearless, they will fight to the end. It would be in proud pursuit of cattle that all Maasai warriors would wish to die if death must come.

On certain occasions when warriors are happy, such as during the rainy season, they hunt lions as a demonstration of bravery and courage. This formal lion hunt is called *alamaiyo*. They also hunt lions when it becomes necessary, if they prey on their herds or when they injure people. When a lion attacks, the warriors respond promptly. They leave the kraal in a hurry, armed with swords and spears. With great determination, they carry out a search until they find the beast and kill it. Sometimes, if they fail to get the one they are after, they will seek revenge by killing any lion they can find.

When warriors go on a formal lion hunt to prove their courage, they follow a set procedure. The day before the hunt, certain warriors spread the word to the others that there will be a hunt the following day and tell them the place to meet. At dawn a warrior with a metal bell tied to his thigh circles all the nearby kraals to remind the warriors of the hunt. When the warriors hear the bell rattle, they dash out fully armed and head to the chosen meeting place. After everyone has arrived, they all discuss which is the best area for the hunt. Once they agree on the most likely place to find the lion, the warriors start out in a long, loose line toward that spot. The lighter and better sprinters are in the front, and those warriors with the heaviest shields will follow behind slowly until the lion is sighted. When a warrior sees a lion, he yells "Eele," and this cry carries all down the line to the last warrior, who, as soon as he hears the cry, responds "Eele" and dashes to the front to catch up with the others. Meanwhile, the warriors in front chase the lion to try to tire him out, for lions always run for their lives when they spot Maasai warriors.

Lions differ in temperament. Some are cowardly and will never tire of running for their lives. Others are proud and will give up running after a few hundred yards and turn around to fight. Certain ones, who have eaten a great deal the night before, are too full of meat to run. These lions will always try to stop and vomit so as to get lighter, and this gives the warriors a chance to try and kill them. Maasai warriors prefer the arrogant, temperamental lions and those full of meat.

When the lion gets mad and decides to fight, the warriors in front slow down to allow those in the rear to catch up. When all the warriors have arrived, they try to circle the lion, at first at a good distance. They sing songs to mesmerize the beast and then close in slowly until they are at a spear-throwing distance. Lions are known for vengefully attacking the warrior who strikes them first. With that in mind, the warriors move in cautiously, until a courageous one decides to spear the lion. After hitting the lion, he runs out of the circle and waits at a distance with his sword in hand. The other warriors barricade the lion's path with shields, throwing spears at him to kill him before he gets to his first attacker. Sometimes they succeed, and sometimes they fail. The lion may be too fast for them and may catch up with the warrior. Even if the warrior has a shield, the lion can usually penetrate it and pin him down.

When the warrior who first spears the lion does so, he must loudly proclaim the name of his family and clan so that all the other warriors will hear him. This ensures that there will be no doubt that the lion belongs to him. The others will repeat the warrior's name among themselves to stop any fights that might occur if another warrior claims he speared the lion first. If all goes well, the warrior who first speared the lion takes its mane and tail, and the second to spear the lion takes its paw. Both stick their trophies onto their spearheads. They perform a symbolic dance around the lion's carcass and then, with triumph, they head home to celebrate. They will celebrate only if none of the warriors in the hunt has been wounded, but even if one has been, they will still take the trophies home to show that they did kill the lion.

Anyone seeing Maasai warriors after a successful lion hunt or cattle raid will always remember the experience. Towering over everyone else, the victorious warriors put on their ceremonial gear— the ostrich plumes on their heads stiffly erect, their headdresses of lion's manes or eagle feathers fiercely proud, and the metal bells on their thighs rattling and bewitching. In this attire they form a procession and head home with pride and confidence. As they set out, they send an emissary before them to inform the warriors at home who did not take part in the victory. They hope by this precaution to ward off any envy or quarrels that sudden news of the victory might bring. The news will set everyone in the home kraals running in different directions, excitedly telling each other, "Warriors have killed a lion! Warriors have killed a lion!" The warriors who remained at home will be sure to meet the victors outside the kraal with the excited frenzy the Maasai call *emboshona*. With praiseful greetings, they will say to the victorious, "Such are the Maasai warriors."

Girls and women alike will run to their houses to decorate themselves and put on their best necklaces and clothes to greet the victorious warriors. The girls, in particular, will try to outdo one another in dressing, because the two most attractive girls will have the chance to dance with the first two warriors to spear the lion. The elders and women will come to the main gates and wait with calabashes of milk to bless the warriors. Soon after the formal greeting, they will all join in a celebration with much singing and milk drinking. If a lioness has been killed, the warriors will

Thigh bell

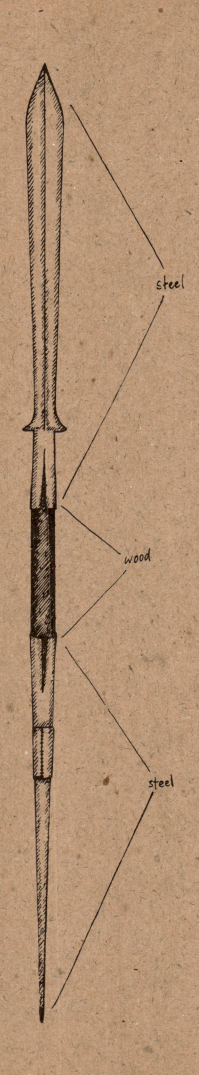

steel

wood

steel

Three-part warrior's spear

have celebrations in four kraals; if a male lion, in eight. The lion is the king of beasts and the only animal whose killing the Maasai celebrate.

The plains and rolling hills of their broad land must have witnessed, many a time, Maasai warriors in action. Their weapons are treacherous—the sharp sword with a double edge used to hit and slash; the short club with a round head used for beating or throwing at the enemy; the stick with sharp points at each end, which is hurled at the enemy; and, indeed, the spear with its invisible thrust, the warrior's best friend. Warriors have various traditional war formations for approaching the enemy, depending on whether he is positioned in open plain, forest, or bush country. If the enemy is in open country, for instance, they close in, carrying enormous buffalo shields, and create a wall of warriors in an eagle-wing formation. The bravest warriors form a spearhead in the center to split and penetrate to the heart of the enemy line. Others will be positioned on the sidelines to give support to the spearhead. Behind the spearhead there is the rear guard, which comes to the rescue in case the front is overpowered.

While Maasai warriors are famous for being unbeatable during battle, they also know how to accept defeat. They will always say, "The war will be won by either side, ours or theirs," as the following song illustrates:

Motonyi ai Motonyi ai e Engai,
God, bird of prey,
Mariamari iltatua lekeri olongoni,
Accompany me on the raid,
Enemenanu etaraki naarisho,
Because if I don't get killed,
Nemeeta kata akeye emotonyi ai Engai
I will kill, and you will always have
Nimeraa enekiri
One of us to feed upon.

Like the male lion, whom he hunts yet respects, the mature Maasai warrior often seeks out the secluded life. He frequently goes to the *olpul*, or feasting camp, in the heart of nature, where he and his comrades can be far away from people's noises. Only the sharp eyes of the crow or raven can see them. The sounds of wooing touracos awaken them in the early morning hours before the dew leaves the trees and the grass. Here, in these forest retreats, Maasai warriors who usually never bother to pray must pray formally to *Engai*. They pray at early dawn, when birds are doing the same. One warrior at a time walks out of the *olpul* carrying a little stick, the symbol of the cattle herder, and prays by speaking directly to God. One common prayer is the following:

Ng'asak Engakenya ai Engai. Naata esirua neeta enanyokie namuru tokino engalepok ooloshon pookin. Atupukuo olamonyak oing'ua iloomonyak ootii elashani, lemearie iloowaarak elalaa nemearie ilmotonyi engararaa, lemewarr emowarak oomunyi nemewarr eremetaa. Engishon Aamon, nayang'oyang'nye naimu olopongi lookeleruani nemerinyo ituabau nemesioyo eyewo. Ebukuoi iloowaarak olmotonyi eng'are nitookutuo amu ekenyikia iyook kiserian. Enjoo iyook engishu ooengera—enjoo iyook tenegum ne'njo teneropa. Enjoo iyook king'oru nenjo miking'oro. Enteshapa iyook engishon anaailtuli, iribie iyook enaa engaik. Entabai iyook iltuli oomokota lekitoo. Sere naa engakenya ai Engai pe kintoki ake atomo too sidan, pee entoki angorie iyook iltiel oomonyak.

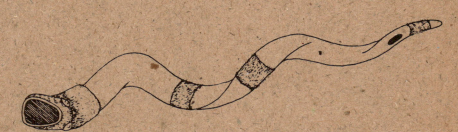

Decorated kudu horn, blown at Eunoto *ceremony*

Greetings, heavenly dawn. You come to us in red and white. Our women compete to greet you. I come here, the blessed of the blessed, still resting beneath the tree. No wild animals, nor vultures' wings will tamper with us. No rhino horns or sharp spearpoints will separate us. I pray for prosperity. Let it come to us in slow, uphill motions. Let it come to stay. Wild beasts and vultures, hush—your expectations were not met, for we are all still alive. Bequeath us babies and cows, on the slopes and on the plains, when we search and when we don't. Give us prosperity by surprise. Keep us until the wrinkles of old age. Goodbye, heavenly dawn, until tomorrow when we shall meet again in peace and in the golden rays of prosperity.

As one warrior finishes his prayer, he walks back to the *olpul* and another leaves to pray. Prayers differ depending on what one is asking for. Like most prayers, they are very personal. In the evening after the warriors have eaten their roasted meat, they recite a prayer of blessing as a group, led by one warrior. As these prayers are said, the thorny entrance to the *olpul* is closed by the warrior leading the prayers.

When the pressure from the generation below them becomes great enough, warriors are forced to graduate into elderhood to make room for the new generation. The most important ceremony involved in this transition is called *Eunoto*, literally, "planting." After much consideration, a suitable site is chosen at which to hold the *Eunoto* ceremony. A special large manyatta is built to accommodate the participants, who include the Maasai elders who must supervise the event. When the manyatta has been completed, a day is chosen for a gathering of all the warriors of the section. To the accompaniment of kudu horns, they arrive in full warrior regalia, their heads covered with ocher, bells on their thighs, and wearing their lion-mane and ostrich feather headdresses and the special multicolored togas called *nangan*. They do not bear weapons, but rather in their place carry long white poles signifying the coming of elderhood.

With the help of elders, the warriors select an *Alaunoni* from among themselves. The *Alaunoni* must be a warrior of great honor with exceptionally good qualities. Since this highly respected individual will clear the path for his generation-mates to enter the new life of elderhood, he must be unblemished in all ways. His background must be of pure Maasai origin, and he must have a large herd of cattle. His physical beauty and health must be perfect. If he has any major defect in his body, such as a blind eye or a crippled limb, he will not be elected. He must never have killed anyone or have association with any stain, such as a curse. His parents must still be alive and be of good repute. The warriors consult a *Laibon* concerning the selection of the *Alaunoni*, and if he is doubtful or does not approve, they have to select another person.

A new sheepskin garment and the coiled brass ornaments called *isurutia*—both Maasai fertility symbols—are fetched and kept until the day of the ceremony. After he is elected, the *Alaunoni* must hang the *isurutia* around his neck and will be often called *oloosurutia*, meaning "the one with *isurutia*." His selection must be kept secret from him until the first day of the ceremony, when people will capture him by surprise and put the *isurutia* on him. If he were told that he was the one chosen, he would run away and hide or find a way to make himself unfit for selection by scarring himself, or hurting someone, or doing something to make himself blemished. Being selected as *Alaunoni*, even though it is a very great honor, is also a heavy responsibility and something every warrior would wish to avoid. The *Alaunoni* represents the entire warrior generation of all Maasai sections, as they move into elderhood.

The warriors and elders select another warrior, called *Alabaroenkeene*, who must be of high honor and whose ox will be sacrificed for the ceremony. The *Alabaroenkeene*, along with the *Alaunoni* and the *Alaigwanani* (who has already been selected during circumcision), will preside over the activities of the ceremony.

The *Eunoto* ceremony itself lasts for four days and involves the building of a special manyatta of forty-nine houses as well as the construction of a ceremonial house, the ritual slaughter and roasting of bullocks to feed the participants, and the shaving of the warriors'

long hair. *Eunoto* is very well attended and there is much singing and dancing between major events. The ceremonial house, called *o-singira*, is built in the center of the manyatta with forty-nine houses. The *o-singira* is round, with a conical roof made of thatch and is totally different from the typical flat-roofed Maasai dwelling. The *o-singira* may be constructed only by those of the warriors' mothers who have not had sexual intercourse with any warriors of their sons' generation. All the food—milk, roasted meat, and honey beer for the elders—will be kept within this house and handed out to participants by the elder-sponsors. The main events of the ceremony revolve around this structure.

After the *o-singira* is constructed, the warriors retreat to a private place by a river, where the elders have prepared *enturoto*. The warriors cover their bodies with this white chalk paint and return to the ceremonial kraal in a long procession, singing. In one of the most sentimental moments of the ceremony, the mother of each warrior shaves off her son's long plaited hair, using a mixture of milk and water to soften it. If a mother has had sexual intercourse with any one of the warriors in her son's generation, she will not be allowed to shave her son's hair, and a close relative will take her place. The *Alaunoni* is the first to be shaved. The warriors being shaved sit on the same cowhide used during their circumcision. If they no longer have the same hide, they must sit on an equally unblemished one. After each warrior is shaved, ocher and animal fat are rubbed onto his head.

Often the warriors will cry or go into an emotional frenzy, shaking all over and foaming at the mouth, desolate at the loss of the beautiful long hair that has been a proud possession during the highest period of their manhood. They hate the idea of their approaching elderhood, which marks the coming of old age and the end of warrior comradeship; they are also displeased if their own mothers did not shave them. After the warriors, particularly the younger ones of the generation, leave the manyatta, they sometimes let their hair grow once again. Those who do not want to let their hair grow, however, are no longer punished with fines of cattle as they used to be by the leaders of the generation.

During the *Eunoto* ceremony, only warriors who have not had sexual intercourse with circumcised women are permitted to enter the *o-singira*. Parents usually linger near the house to check whether their sons are among those who abstain, for this would tell them straight away that their sons' conduct had fallen below the expected norm. If a warrior enters the *o-singira* and has committed a sexual offense, it is believed by the whole society that he will be cursed and die. If he enters and nothing happens, his behavior will be regarded as honorable and he will be presented with cattle by his clansmen.

At the end of the ceremony, the *Alaunoni* is presented with a girl from a highly reputable family whom he will take as his wife after the ceremony. This is one of the occasions when, regardless of the girl's previous engagement, every marriage custom is put aside. The *Alaunoni* is obliged to marry whichever girl they choose for him, and if she has been betrothed to another warrior, the other warrior must give her up as a duty to society. This final presentation of the girl symbolizes a new phase for all the warriors; they are in transition to becoming elders and are henceforth permitted to marry. The members of the specially built manyatta disperse, and the manyatta is abandoned.

There are two additional smaller ceremonies necessary to pave the way to elderhood: the milk-drinking ceremony and the meat-eating ceremony. In the milk-drinking ceremony, called *Eewokoto Ekole*, each warrior is given milk by the elders. This gesture is interpreted as granting him permission to start drinking milk in the absence of other warriors, thereby breaking the taboo on a warrior's drinking milk without another warrior present. This ceremony takes place in the individual warrior's home, and a sheep is slaughtered and eaten by the family and friends to mark the occasion.

The second and more significant ceremony is *Enginasataa Oongiri*, the communal meat-eating ceremony. This is the last of the ceremonies undergone by the warriors in their transition to junior elderhood. In this ceremony, for the first time since he became a warrior, the man may eat meat in the presence of a circumcised woman. If the man is married, his wife prepares the meat and serves it to him. If he is not, another wife of his generation can feed him the meat, but only if she has conformed to the Maasai sexual laws, particularly in not having sex with any of the new warriors below her husband's generation. Those women who have committed adultery with the new warriors must identify themselves on the ceremonial day by painting their faces one-half white and the other half black. Those who have not committed adultery paint their faces one-half white and the other half red.

The actual ceremony takes place in one day, but has taken about a month to prepare. It is supervised and conducted by the senior elders, and at times there may be more than a thousand participants. Much honey beer is brewed and many oxen slaughtered to satisfactorily feed the many people who attend. As in most Maasai ceremonies, there is a great deal of singing and dancing. Those partaking in the meat-eating ceremony will sing in a separate area from the spectators, since there are many activities which they must undergo as a group, such as being continuously blessed by elders with the words, "Prosper, rest, have children, have cattle." It is an amazing sight to see almost one thousand people following and responding to blessings in unison.

At the close of the ceremony, the participants leave the kraal singing, in procession, and reenter through the main gate, moving slowly in long lines. On either side of the entrance, which is decorated with sacred palm branches, two elders stand. They anoint each person as he passes through with the fat of an unblemished sheep, splashing it on his face and his stomach as well. Barren women are also brought to this ceremony to receive the communal blessings of the elders of their generation so they may bear children. The rest of the spectators will be singing, while those who prefer not to sing, senior elders in particular, will be drinking milk or honey beer and eating meat. The meat-eating ceremony takes place in one day of intense activity, and by sunset all is completed. The new elders then disperse to their homes to face the challenges and growing responsibilities of elderhood.

To become a warrior is
the dream of every Maasai youth; the word itself
seems to convey magical powers. A warrior must be
strong, clever, courageous, confident, wise,
and gentle. He must hunt lions for his
headdress, protect his herds from predators, retrieve
stolen or strayed cattle, often from long distances,
and safeguard his community. Warriors enjoy
great comradeship, sharing with one another everything
from food to girl friends. In addition to the practical
services they provide for the group they live among,
warriors also add an immeasurable sense of
excitement, adventure, and romance; without their
songs, their poetry, their flirting, their bold masculinity,
Maasai life would not be the same.

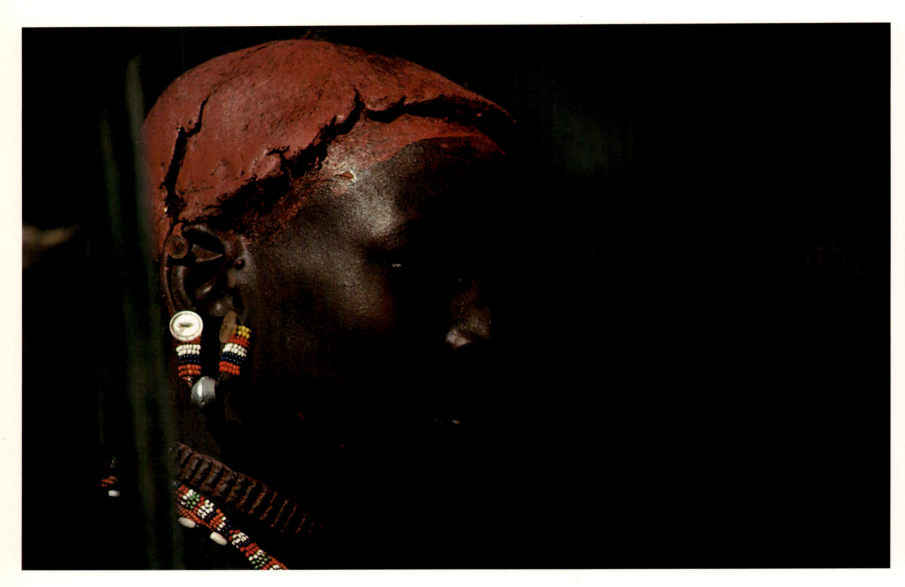

The young warrior begins to grow his hair long and to
put on the heavy ocher make-up and ornamentation that
particularly mark his warriorhood. Colorful beads, buttons,
and metal objects adorn his earlobes. Bead necklaces
fashioned by girl friends crisscross his chest. Around his
neck he wears a special neckband made from a goat's
stomach lining; fragrant seeds are pressed into a strip of
the lining while it is still wet and are tied in place with
string. Attached to the neckband at the throat is a disk
made from the shell of a crocodile egg.

Warriors spend a great deal of time styling their hair. The hair is first dressed with animal fat and ocher and then parted across the top of the head at ear level. The basic plaiting involves parting the hair into small sections, dividing each section in two, and then twisting each part, first separately and then together. Cotton or wool threads are twisted in to lengthen the hair. Plaited hair may hang loose (*following pages*) or be gathered together and bound with leather.

The warrior's other major body decoration is leg painting. Coating his legs with ocher, he creates patterns by drawing his fingertips through the wet color, exposing the dark skin.

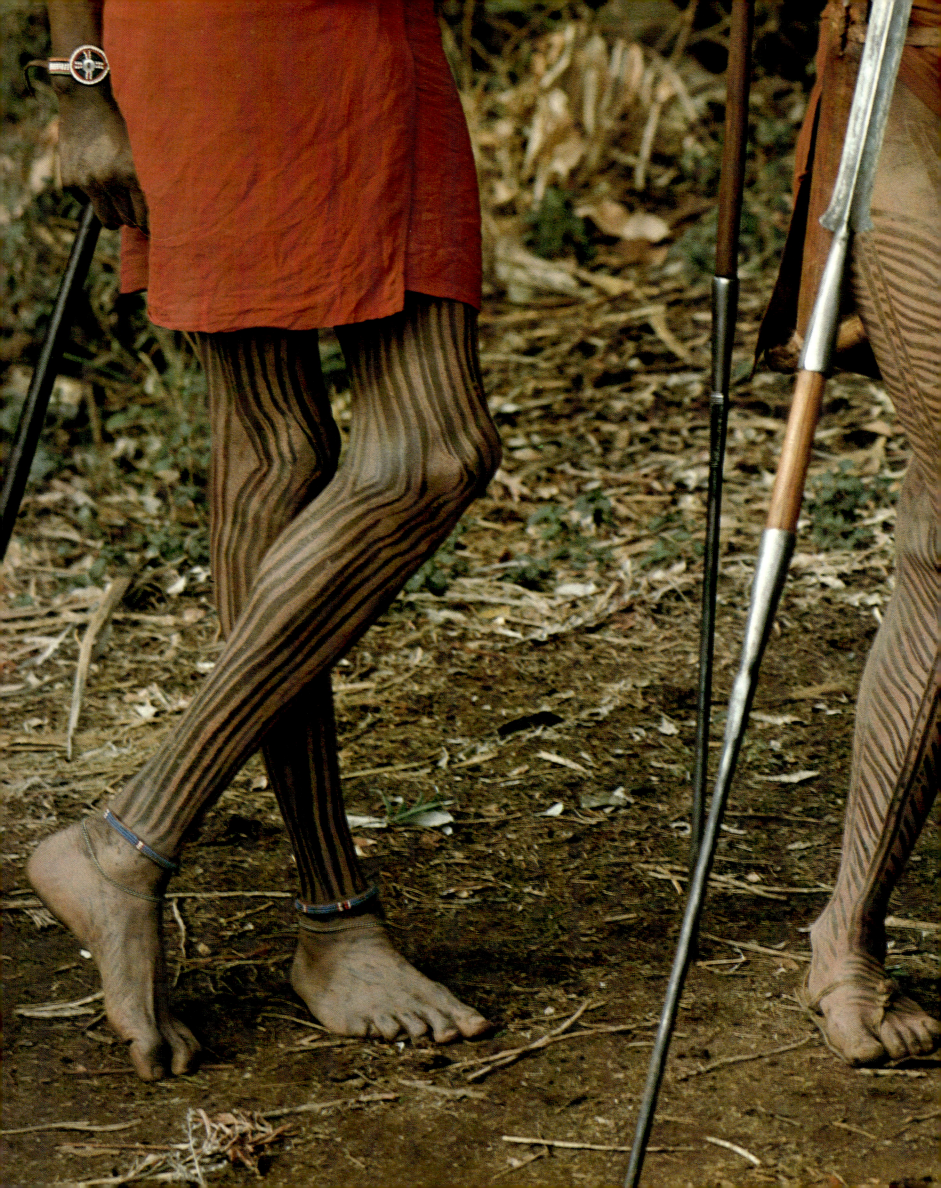

Beaded decorations are the most common ornaments worn by Maasai men and women alike. One Maasai dictionary lists some forty different words for specific types of beadwork. Among the wide variety of beaded decorations worn by warriors—on their heads, around their necks, at their ears, on their arms and legs—is a narrow belt that serves to carry the scabbard of the short sword. The belt is often embellished at the back with a pattern sewn on a leather form. All warrior beads are fashioned by women, most by girl friends; anklets or upper-arm bands are particular signs of love. Worn for long periods, they may be given as gifts or exchanged man to man.

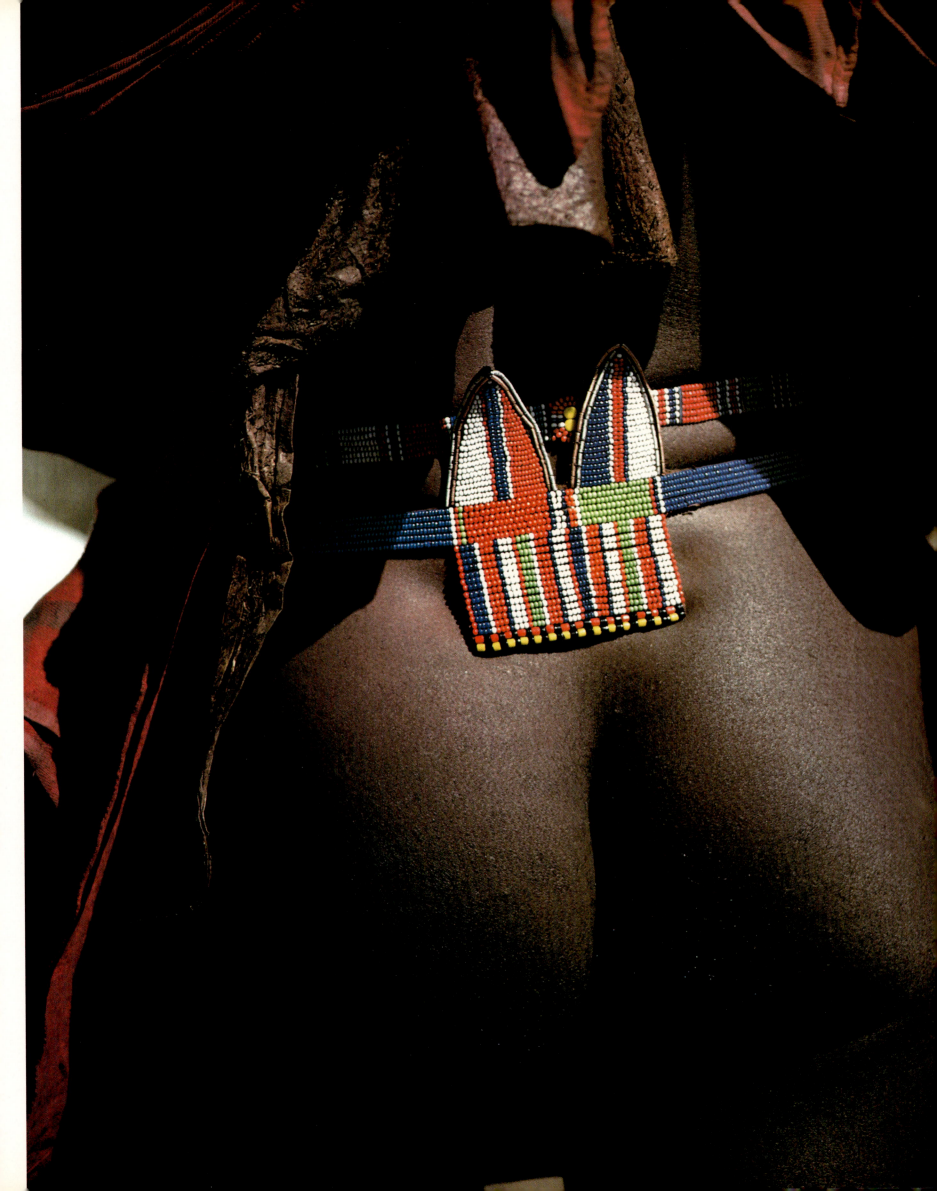

During their years as warriors, Maasai males often retreat to a feasting camp called *olpul,* deep in the bush, far from the presence of women. There, they gain strength, share warrior wisdom and lore, and prepare for lion hunts and cattle raids. The feasting itself begins with the suffocation of an ox, lamb, or goat. The animal's neck is slit and the blood that collects there is drunk while still warm. The underbelly is cut, and the heart, kidneys, and liver are removed and eaten. The skin is pulled off and the meat to be roasted is stretched on pliant branches shaped into "kites" and placed by the fire. Fatty parts are kept in a hide container and are later made into a meat soup. A second broth, believed to give courage, is

brewed from acacia bark and blended into the meat soup with a twirled stick to break down the fat.

After their solitary *olpul,* warriors return home to their girl friends, to flirt and play games, chasing each other with long, leafy branches, and conducting mock jousts. They also play among themselves, running races, practicing spear throwing, and dodging hurled sisal stalks with their shields. At day's end the warriors and girls come together to sing and dance. Both traditional and original songs form the repertoire. Unaccompanied by instruments, the male and female dancers move to repetitive, throaty vocal rhythms, usually uttered by the males, and to solo melodies, delivered by the best singers.

Maasai men will frequently take part in jumping dances, competing for height but always displaying a sense of effortlessness. They gather in a circle and sing with a strong, breathy beat. One or two of them move into the center of the circle and jump rhythmically, embellishing their leaps by subtly trembling their shoulders at the peak of the jump.

The major ceremony of warrior life, called *Eunoto,* marks the transition to elderhood, when a man may marry. Preparations take months; lions are hunted for manes and ostrich feathers gathered to make headdresses; kudu-horn trumpets are decorated with lion tails. At a site and on a date chosen by the chief *Laibon,* the warriors' mothers construct a large manyatta. From distant feasting camps, hundreds of warriors march to the site. As they approach, to the accompaniment of kudu horns and with their metal thigh bells jingling, many become crazed with emotion. They may go rigid, thrust out their arms, froth at the mouth, and utter repetitive animal-like sounds. Their mothers and other warriors calm them.

Next morning, the warriors, wearing cloaks of Kanga cloth around their shoulders, perform the *Enkipaata* dance to horn and voice. They charge wildly around the manyatta in small groups, at intervals falling to their knees, waving their headdresses in unison.

Following *Enkipaata,* the forty-nine mothers whose sons are held to be the most distinguished build a second manyatta of forty-nine hide houses. At its center they construct the *o-singira,* a house for the most sacred rituals. Those warriors who have not had sexual relations with circumcised women may enter the *o-singira* to spend the night drinking milk and receiving a variety of special blessings.

At one point in *Eunoto,* the warriors perform a special ceremony in honor of their mothers. A white ox is roasted at the center of the manyatta. The mothers seat themselves in a large circle, and a select group of warriors distribute chunks of the best meat to them. While doing so, the warriors tease and flirt with them, calling them women rather than mothers. The men's calls are full of good-natured sexual innuendo and playful joking.

Throughout this ceremony, small groups of warriors may be found outside the manyatta decorating their bodies with ocher, slathering it on generously and often drawing complex patterns with their fingertips.

167

One of the most emotional moments of *Eunoto* involves
the shaving of the warriors' beautiful long, plaited hair.
At dawn, mothers and sons gather beside their houses;
the mother anoints her son's head with milk, and slowly
and carefully scrapes it bald. As the long plaits fall, each
warrior seems to experience a great sadness.

It is a mark of honor for a mother to prepare her son
for elderhood in this way, and only a woman who has
refrained from sexual relations with the warriors of her
son's generation may shave her son's head. When all the
heads are shaved, each is freshly ochered, and the
warriors gather to sing and dance, sharing their
memories of warriorhood.

Early the next morning, the warriors march to a sacred mountain for secret rituals and further blessings by their elder sponsors.

On the final day of *Eunoto*, the warriors gather again in a large circle at the center of the manyatta for a series of blessings by the elders. First, they receive draughts of milk from special calabashes decorated with cowrie shells. Then the elders paint them with white chalk; circles are drawn on their faces, and long lines trace the lengths of their bodies, arms, and legs. When each warrior has been so blessed, all gather together in the center and seat themselves on the ground. The elder-sponsors circle the group and as a final blessing spit mouthfuls of honey beer onto the new junior elders. After listening to various words of counsel from their sponsors, they leave the manyatta and return home.

176

Ilpayiani: Elders

"Now that you are an elder drop your weapons and use your head and wisdom instead." "Master the art of the tongue and wisdom of mind." "Family responsibility rests on your shoulders." Such words echo in the mind of a Maasai as he embarks on the new life of elderhood. The new junior elder prepares himself for his new role in many ways, his first concern being marriage. As the time for elderhood draws near, while he is still a senior warrior, he begins to pay great attention to his prospective father-in-law. Bearing presents, he makes frequent visits to the home of his betrothed to demonstrate to the in-laws his great desire to marry their daughter. He is also careful to show great respect to the senior elders who supervise the new generation of elders since, should this respect fall short, he could be fined. Only after paying these elders the fine of a heifer or a brew of honey beer will he be allowed to marry one of their daughters. At certain times, elders will take advantage of this needy period in a junior elder's life and will punish him for his past misbehavior, for refusing to obey senior elders' requests, for instance. The junior elders, wanting so much to get married, are very vulnerable.

Now that the comradeship of warriorhood has passed, a junior elder seeks a place to settle down and a life partner, or partners, since polygamy is allowed in Maasailand. The senior elders, besides demanding dowries for their daughters, want to make sure that the prospective husbands can support their daughters. Believing that "He who loves cattle and works hard will always get them," the elders prefer and trust a suitor who has many cattle over one who has few. So, although most marriages are arranged at an early age, if the father of the daughter finds a more suitable husband for her at a later time, he may dissolve the first arrangement. Of course, there are always some families who, out of loyalty and pride, will stick with the first son-in-law regardless.

A Maasai girl may be betrothed during infancy, and sometimes even before. When the parents of a son see a newly wedded couple, they may give the young couple a brass ring or chain necklace and ask that any daughter they should beget may become the wife of their son. They wait until they hear that the couple has been blessed with a daughter, and then, without wasting time, they will come to reaffirm their old claim by giving the child's mother a fat sheep for slaughter. They continue to give presents until the daughter comes of age. If the girl's family continues to accept their presents, the chances of the girl's becoming their son's wife are good. Rejection of the presents at any time indicates a change of attitude on the part of the girl's family.

Following the girl's circumcision, the husband-to-

At left:
Naikosiai, the author's brother, surveys his
herd at dawn on the day he will undergo a ceremony
enabling him to initiate his children—
a proud achievement.

be becomes more eager to marry and comes to demand her, bringing to her family the necessary articles of tobacco, honey, or a heifer. If these articles are accepted, she is then wedded and leaves her kraal to go to live in her husband's.

Another method of betrothal is one often used by *Laibon* families. When a man meets a girl and grows to like her, he puts a metal chain around her neck, symbolizing his interest in marriage. News of this spreads quickly through the kraal, and the girl's parents await the arrival of the man to declare his intentions openly. In the meantime, the man will obtain some honey, which he will bring to his mother. She and another woman of his clan take this honey, together with some milk, to the home of the girl's parents. This gift of honey acts as a declaration of interest in marriage and is known as *esiret e nkoshoke* ("honey to mark the stomach"). It is not brewed into beer but is instead eaten by the women of the bride's household. At a later time before the marriage, a greater quantity of honey is supplied and once again carried with milk to the home of the girl's parents. This honey, called *enkiroret* ("honey for discussion"), is brewed into beer, and the father of the bride then invites his relatives and the other elders of his generation to come together over the honey beer to discuss the merits of the proposed son-in-law.

When the beer has been drunk, the man who has declared his interest is summoned and informed whether his proposal is acceptable or not. If it has been accepted, the suitor and the bride's family begin a long and close relationship. If, on the other hand, the proposal has been rejected, the entire matter is thereafter forgotten and the suitor does not attempt to recover the cost of the *enkiroret*. Any other gifts he has given to the family, such as goats or sheep, will, however, be returned to him. (There is a third form of betrothal in Maasailand in which one young man may decide to take another man's sister as his wife and, in return, gives his own sister to be married to that man.)

No matter what method of betrothal is followed, after a suitor is accepted by the girl's family, he gives them as many gifts as he can afford. As the gifts are accepted, they go to make up her required dowry, and are also assurances to the suitor that thenceforth no one may try to marry the girl. The dowry is more a means to legalize the marriage than to bring in wealth. The traditional dowry is five animals and three articles: two heifers, one steer, one ram, one ewe, tobacco, honey, and two sheepskins (counted as one). One of the heifers must be given by the young man to the girl's father, and thereafter they will call each other *pakiteng* or *entawuo* ("cow" or "heifer") in remembrance of the gift. The ewe is given to the girl's mother by the

young man, and they will likewise greet each other with the word *paker* ("ewe"). The ram is slaughtered and some of its fat is mixed with ocher to be used for body paint in ceremonies. The rest is put into a container which the bride carries with her on her back to her new home. The two sheepskins are given to the girl's mother, who will make a dress from them. Some clans allow the couple to marry before the total dowry is paid, while others will not let their daughters leave until it has been entirely paid.

As the time for the wedding approaches, the bride is usually advised by her parents how to behave toward her husband. She is told, "From now on you leave the comfort of your own family. You will no longer be treated as a baby. You are now a person to be relied on, and we expect you to give rather than to receive. You must respect your husband and follow his dictates. If you don't he will beat you, and we give him that permission. Don't run home each time you have a disagreement with your husband unless the situation is serious and you really think you have been mistreated." In return, the girl's mother tells the husband-to-be how to treat her daughter and what her temperament is like. Her father gives him the advice, "Take my daughter, and treat her fairly. Don't let her come running home complaining of your mistreatment. It will be difficult to get her back."

A Maasai wedding is very colorful. The bride wears a long garment made of the softest and most beautifully tanned sheepskin. Around the edges and center of the wedding garment, the mother of the bride and the other women of the community have sewn multicolored beads in intricate patterns. The bride is adorned with many bead necklaces, the most magnificent of all being the *entente*, a wedding necklace made of long, straight links of beads reaching to the knees. Rich families buy expensive silver wire to be coiled like stockings around the bride's legs. This decoration is called *isenkenke olkiteng*. Everything worn by the bride must be new and shiny with much ocher.

The actual marriage ceremony is simple. The bride's head is shaved and anointed with lamb fat, and bands of beautiful beadwork are placed around her head. The bride and groom are both blessed and washed with milk, and green grass is tied onto their shoes and clothes. After drinking the honey beer brewed from the suitor's presents, the bride's father and his age-mates wish the couple prosperity and many children. As her mother and the other community women lead the bride outside the kraal, she will be crying as a demonstration that she is sad to be leaving her family. She is warned not to look back toward her family's kraal until she has reached her husband's place, for it is believed that if she does she will turn into stone out of grief for what she is leaving behind. When the escorting women return to their kraal, the bride is left walking very, very slowly with her new husband and the best man, who clears her path by removing any sticks or thorns that might be in her way. If there is a river to be crossed, the best man will be the one to lift her across. Before she will talk to her husband or enter his kraal or his family's house, the bride must receive gifts. Each member of her new family, her husband's father, mother, brother, sisters, and even his friends, gives her a present of livestock. The wealth of gifts she receives depends on how large the family is. When she is satisfied, she enters her new house, which at first is the house of her husband's mother. For two days, until her head is shaved by her husband's mother, the new bride will not sleep with her husband nor will her husband eat food from the house she is staying in. Later on, the new bride will build a house of her own.

When a Maasai man gets married, his first wife will build her house on the right side of the main gate to his kraal, and his second will occupy the left side, creating two equal "pillars." When another marriage follows, the new wife will go right and the next wife left, and so on in this order. The first wife retains seniority in kraal affairs, but she may not necessarily command the husband's affection. The *enkirotet*, or favorite wife, can be any of the women, depending on how they relate to the husband, and the same applies to the *endingi*, the least favored wife. Jealousy among Maasai women does exist, but the husband will always try to see that each wife has her fundamental needs met. If any of these needs, such as having his children and being given food and protection, are not fulfilled a wife can return to her parents.

In Maasai tradition, the husband is the head of the family. While the wife is responsible for running the household, she has very little say in making major decisions. A wife must respect her husband. Although a husband disciplines his wife and even sometimes beats her, he must always have good reasons or else she will run away to her parents or clan relatives and it will be difficult to get her back. A wife will always try to give her husband as many children as she can, because of the importance of children in Maasailand. With children, a man's cattle will be well taken care of and his name will live forever. A man may marry as many wives as he wishes, and a married woman may have lovers. A woman may even have children by a lover, but the children will always belong to her husband. While it is acceptable to have children by other men, it is a matter of great pride to have children who resemble one's husband. Therefore, women will see to it that during their fertile times they are with

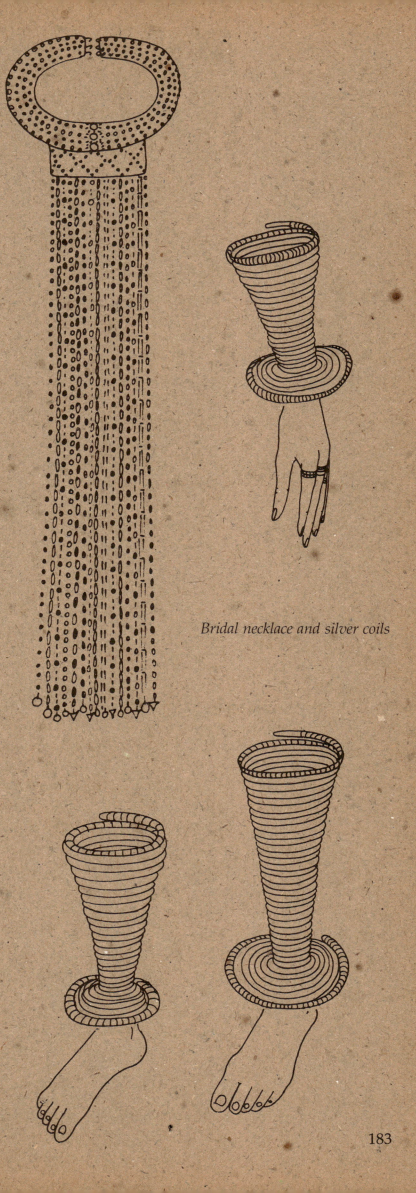

Bridal necklace and silver coils

183

their husbands and not with their lovers.

Except in unusual circumstances, there is no divorce in Maasailand. The reason for this is that the Maasai find it extremely difficult to break and dissolve the bond that the marriage has created between the two families. In addition, the repayment of the dowry is a complex matter. The Maasai always try to bring the husband and wife back together by convening a council of elders for a serious discussion of the situation and particularly of who is most to blame. The elders will then reprimand the party they think is in the wrong and will warn him or her not to repeat the offense again. If the woman is in the wrong, she may be reprimanded verbally or beaten. If the man happens to be the one who was too cruel to his wife and if he will not listen to the elders' advice, his wife will be taken away from him and sent back to her father's house. The wife's clan will have to repay the dowry, and the wife may then be given away to another man. If the wife in such a case has given birth to children, the dowry need not be repaid because the children will take its place; in accordance with tradition, they will remain in the man's custody.

Junior elders must go through two major rituals before they settle down totally into elderhood. The first of these is called *Olngesherr* and is an endorsement of complete elderhood. At this ceremony, the elders are given a new group name that permanently marks their generation. One such name, for instance, might be *Ilmeshuki*, meaning "Those never defeated in war." Every section of Maasailand undergoes this ceremony, passing the name from section to section.

The main features of this complex ceremony are as follows. An unblemished ox is selected and killed by suffocation. Its dewlap is slit, and the blood that collects within it is mixed with milk and honey beer and drunk by each elder undergoing the ceremony. The elders' wives then construct a ceremonial fence of animal hides. The meat of the ox is roasted within this enclosure, and the participants in the ceremony all gather inside the fence to eat the meat. Before they do, certain parts of the meat—the chest, for one—are rubbed on their foreheads as a blessing. The following morning, further blessings of sour milk in well-cleaned gourds are bestowed on the elders. Each one is also given a new ring made from the underbelly of the slain ox. As an added benediction, white ceremonial paint is splashed on the face of each new elder by the senior elders.

A striking feature of *Olngesherr* ceremony involves the blessing of the cattle sticks of the newly confirmed elders. Their branding irons are first anointed with ghee and honey and put into a fire. When they are heated, they are plunged into a pool of cow urine. As the heated irons meet the cool liquid, a smoky vapor rises. The elders wave their cattle sticks in the smoke, blessing them in this way. *Olngesherr* ceremony ends with the stretching of the ceremonial oxhide and the planting of a green shoot by a revered elder at each entrance to the manyatta.

The second major ritual of elderhood is named *Olkiteng Lorrbaa*, literally, "ox to inflict injuries." This is a purification ceremony whereby all of the elder's past misdeeds are forgiven. Each elder must undergo this ceremony individually in order to be allowed to initiate his children into manhood or womanhood when the time comes. *Olkiteng Lorrbaa* involves the slaughter of an unblemished ox, provided by the elder, and the roasting and eating of its meat. This ceremony is famous for its mock fighting between the men and women. In the late afternoon, a skewer of raw meat is placed in the middle of a field, and a competition then takes place between the men and women for possession of the skewer. One group charges at the other, waving leafy branches in an effort to chase it away from the skewer, for the group that pushes the other away will take the skewer in victory. The fighting, all in good fun, is exciting to watch because it really gets heated. This being a rare chance for women to whip their husbands, the women take full advantage of the opportunity, and they often win. Swift Maasai women, sticks raised over their shoulders, will dash up to the elders and whip them. When they discover a particularly vigorous and brave elder, three or four women will gang up on him and not leave until he takes to his heels or begs for mercy.

Soon after the battle has been won and the skewer taken away by the winning side, all come together to sing and dance. They march to the kraal entrance and sing until the cattle return from pasture. Holding ceremonial calabashes filled with milk and grass, the junior elder undergoing the ceremony and his first wife wait at the cattle entrance and bless the herd as it enters the kraal. In the evening the elder is escorted to his mother's house by an elder of his age-group who is "unblemished," that is, one who has never had a brother die and who has never killed a person himself. Joined by other elders inside the house, the elder and his escort eat a special piece of meat prepared by the elders from the chest of the ox. All of the elders drink honey beer, bless the one undergoing the ceremony and sing to him, practically throughout the night.

While drinking, the elders sing songs celebrating fierce bulls and beautiful oxen and the women they loved when they were young. After the women have fed their children, they join in singing alongside their men. The Maasai live their lives fully from day to day and do not regret when they come of age. They always say that they had the best when they were young but are ready for whatever is in store for them, even death.

Elders are the family men, wise men, medicine men, spiritual advisers, and judges of Maasai society. Guardians of its laws and spiritual mores, they take pride in being the conscience of society and strive always to live up to that responsibility. All decisions regarding the welfare of Maasailand are made by the elders, who must be disciplined and hardworking. They give advice to young men on all kinds of matters; they mediate disputes and decide upon serious punishments. They see to it that harmonious links between different generations and clans are maintained and perpetuated. Indeed, they are the wisdom behind the different pillars of the society.

The elders organize and lead religious functions and ceremonies such as *Alamal Lengipaata*, the ritual performed by boys just before circumcision. While the *Laibon* presides over these ceremonies and helps by providing lucky charms, it is the community elders who supervise the process, give advice, and see to it that all the ceremonial requirements are followed and properly carried out. After all, it is dangerous to mishandle a religious rite or not to perform one at the necessary time. In such cases, the Maasai believe, bad luck in the form of disease, famine, or cattle deaths will befall the whole generation.

Maasai elders are known for their eloquence of speech as well as for their love of truth. During their meetings, one group of elders will sometimes move away from the rest for a private discussion, known as *engilepata*, to consider the most effective way of presenting their views. The Maasai's grace in speaking often impressed the colonial authorities in earlier times. Since they love fine speech, elders have a store of proverbs and sayings. Some, indeed, can hardly complete a sentence without one. A few favorites are: *Metigiran engeju metii emorloo*, literally, "A leg cannot gallop without a muscle" (One cannot resolve issues without ability); *Mengor olekutuk inkulukuok*, literally, "He who talks misses no target" (Bad things spoken are bound to happen); *Epolos engiok enaimin*, literally, "The ear penetrates darkness, an eye cannot" (Even in darkness the ear hears).

Stories are told of how the wisdom and fine words of Maasai elders have even disarmed enemies:

There was once an elder who had quarreled with a warrior for some reason or other. The warrior wanted to fight the elder, and so armed himself with all the necessary weapons used to confront a

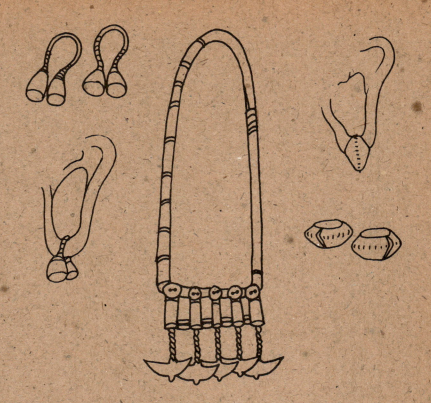

Elders' necklace and ear ornaments

Snuff containers

man—a spear, a club, a sword, and even a shield. The elder was armed only with his wisdom and the long pilgrim's staff he used to support himself as he walked. The elder was seated alone, contemplating the seriousness of the situation. The warrior came along and, without wasting time, lifted his club up high, ready to strike the elder. Luckily enough, the elder saw the shadow of the club looming above his head. Without making any movement, the elder said, "Go ahead and strike, young man, but strike hard enough to stop the flow of words. Yes, the noble truth. After all, isn't that what you are afraid of?" When the young man heard these words, his stick froze in midair and never came down. The elder commanded the young man to leave, saying, "The stick that can strike the truth must be bigger than the one in your hand."

The elders expect, and at times demand, obedience and respect from their juniors. If a person does not greet them properly, refuses to carry out their requests, or, more seriously, has sexual relations with one of their wives, he is punished by having to pay a fine to the elder, consisting of honey beer or perhaps a heifer. If he fails to do this, he is cursed by the elder, a feared occurrence among the Maasai. "May you die on the plain." "May accident come your way." "May the calves of your cattle die"—such curses may be used by anyone, but are most often employed by elders, who have no other weapon. While the warriors have physical strength and spears, the elders are left only with wisdom and their tongues. Most elders seldom abuse the privilege of cursing and, besides, a curse cannot be effective if one does not deserve it. One knowing he has been cursed by an elder usually brews honey beer and then summons other elders of the same age-set to discuss and settle the conflict. After a fine of a heifer is paid, the elders drink the honey beer and ask the offended elder to forgive the offender, who is warned severely not to repeat such an act again. When all the discussion is over, they bless the offender in unison and remove the curse.

Although a rich elder may be influential during decision-making, real prestige among the Maasai is derived from the personality of the individual. There are many admired and influential elders of modest resources. While wealth of cattle and children is reasonably important, qualities of wisdom, intelligence, and modesty are what command real admiration. Elders attain seniority through age: the older they get, the more respect they command, unless they are too deaf or senile to reason well.

The most respected and feared of Maasai elders is

the *Laibon*. He combines the functions of spiritual leader, diviner, healer, expert on rituals, provider of charms and medicines, and adviser to society, in particular to warriors concerning their ceremonies.

The *Laibon* is believed to have descended from God, the story of his origin being as follows:

Two Maasai warriors, who happened to be traveling in a forest, came upon a small child all by himself. One warrior, of the Ilmolelian clan, saw the baby first and wanted to leave him behind. The Ilaiser warrior, however, picked up the child and brought him home with him, subsequently making him his son. (That is why every *Laibon* belongs to the Ilaiser clan.) The boy proved to be of unusual power. For example, when he was sent to tend cattle they always came home well fed, even during times of drought. He was seen to cause rain to fall in front of the herds he was grazing, making the grass grow instantly. Realizing his special powers, the people made him their spiritual leader. He became the first *Laibon*, and his name was Kidongoi. His position has been hereditary ever since.

The most famous *Laibon* in Kenya today is Simel. He officiates over all major Maasai ceremonies in Kenya, grants charms, and foretells the future by using a system of lucky and unlucky numbers. He pours stones out from a calabash or cow horn and uses a complex method of allocating and counting the stones. He repeats this process often, praying, begging, and spitting into the calabash, beseeching his great *Laibon* ancestors, Batiany and Nelion, to aid him.

After being advised to use the art of the tongue and wisdom of mind in place of the spear, junior elders sharpen their newly acquired weapons by attending meetings with the old and experienced elders. Sometimes they travel many miles to attend these meetings, particularly when they know there will be especially wise elders or famous speakers attending them. Travelers through Maasailand often see these impressive groups of elders meeting under an umbrella of acacia trees. They will deliberate all day long until they reach a decision suitable to all the parties concerned. Such meetings are open to every Maasai, and even guests passing through are allowed to sit and listen and are free to contribute.

The elders constitute an impartial body which runs Maasai governmental affairs, maintains justice, and deals with the important issues that enable a society to exist and flourish. Such activities require a great deal of discussion, and every elder has the right to have his say. Few let that privilege pass them by. Custom is their constitution, and most elders keep to it and understand it surely. Feared and respected by the generation below them, elders depend on knowledge, oratory, and wisdom to protect and preserve the Maasai way of living.

The subjects dealt with at elders' meetings range from day-to-day problems, such as the theft of a goat, to more complex issues, such as questions of inheritance and cases of murder. When an individual has a problem, he takes it to a well-known and influential elder or relative. If the elder finds that the problem requires a meeting of elders, he sends warriors to call the elders and spread the word that a meeting will be convened. After all the elders have arrived, a blessing such as "God help us resolve these issues" is spoken, and the elder who called the meeting then opens it by explaining the nature of the problem. If the problem involves two parties, each side will be given an opportunity to present its case. One by one, each elder will then stand to present his views on the case. The elders do not vote, but rather depend on the fact that, after every elder with an opinion has spoken, a consensus will become obvious. The chief of the elders, the *Alaigwanani*, summarizes the conclusion of the elders and states the fine as set down by Maasai law or, in some cases, as decided by the elders' present. The meeting is closed with a blessing such as "We hope we have judged fairly. God bless us all."

While the Maasai elders' courts pass judgments, they have no jails and never inflict any physical punishment, only punishment through fines. Of all things the Maasai hate, the most loathsome to them is human humiliation. Of justice, they always say, "Do one thing—either kill the guilty one or let him live." Most Maasai crimes have prescribed fixed fines. For instance, if someone steals a goat or sheep and is caught, he must pay a two-year-old calf. This same fine also applies to anyone who touches or eats the meat of the stolen animal. If an individual has stolen an animal or taken part in eating it and confesses before he is caught, he may ask forgiveness, saying *Muro* ("Mercy"). He may then pay only one-half of the required fine; for example, if he has stolen a goat or a sheep he may pay only one small ewe. Any animal stolen among the Maasai is always slaughtered, never kept, as the animal would soon be recognized by its markings. For the theft of a cow, the fine is more severe. The thief must pay seven cows, but if the cow is pregnant it will be more, because the baby in the womb is taken into account.

The fine for breaking another person's bones is determined according to the number of bones broken. The fine for one bone—or one tooth, which is counted as one bone—is usually one ewe. If a murder is committed, the guilty party will first hide from the relatives of the deceased until they have calmed down, because they will always try to revenge the murder by killing the offender. When he comes out of hiding, the offender will want to immediately pay the fine of forty-nine cattle specified for a murder. This is because the Maasai believe that one will never be at peace nor will one prosper as long as such a debt has not been paid. Those taking the cattle will come fully armed, as if ready for battle, and will pick the cattle themselves, ensuring that all the cattle are in proper health, none blind or with broken horns.

Cases involving killings are often complex and require much patience and wisdom from the elders. Such cases are rare in Maasailand, however, since Maasai seldom intentionally kill one another. Most involve accidents, such as a child wounding or killing another while playing at throwing spears, or warriors fighting and hurting each other accidentally. Strict regulations govern fighting. When people begin fighting they must first use sticks or clubs, and only if the sticks or clubs break may they use swords, but not to slash. They may nick each other's skin to inflict pain, but it is totally forbidden to slash at each other because that can kill. When spears become necessary in a fight, one must not strike at the soft part of the body, as this can bring instant death, but rather should aim at the person's legs.

In wartime, when Maasai are fighting with non-Maasai, the laws are totally different. During a real war with people of another tribe, they fight to kill, to eliminate their enemies before they themselves are eliminated. If they are victorious, the Maasai do not kill women or young children. They will kill all grown-up males and spirited young men, to prevent their eventual revenge, and will capture all young females and children and marry the females. (The last major Maasai war was fought by the Tanzanian Maasai against the Bantu tribes around Lake Victoria during World War I. The Maasai were aware that the Germans and British rulers of East Africa were preoccupied with the war and were not in a position to stop intertribal warfare. They were most successful in their main purpose, which was to gain cattle to build up their decimated herds.)

When they judge murder cases, the Maasai elders address themselves not only to the victim but to the society as a whole. While they must punish the offender, they will say that the society has already lost one man and cannot afford to lose another. They must be careful not to punish the society, which did not commit the crime. To execute the offender would be to reduce the size and strength of the society, so they

Wildebeeste-tail fly whisk and tobacco container,
prized possessions of elders

usually try to find a way to punish him without hurting the society. There was a case in which two Maasai were taking cattle to market:

On the way to market one of the two men was attacked by a poisonous snake, and he died. When the body was found, it had disintegrated so much that it was difficult to tell if it was his companion or a snake that had killed the man. After much deliberation and with little evidence, the elders decided that the dead man's companion had killed him and that forty-nine blood cattle must be paid by the man, as is customary in Maasai law. The accused man paid the required cattle with a protest to the family of the deceased. As the cattle were being driven away to the deceased man's kraal, they passed the area where the man was attacked and killed by the snake. A snake—perhaps not the actual snake that had killed the man—barricaded the path and prevented the cattle from proceeding, even after several attempts were made to scare it away. The cattle were returned to the owner by the family and, after another consultation, the elders agreed now that it was the snake that had killed the man, and not his companion.

This is how complex Maasai cases can be at times, and the good thing is that the Maasai are aware of both sides, the spirit and the letter of the law. There have been cases that, after failing to be decided by British law, were returned to be judged by traditional methods. Most parts of Maasailand, however, seldom report murders or even minor cases to governmental authority, because they are afraid that the government sees only the legal side and not the important human elements. The following story tells of one such case:

There was a very strict man known by the name of Loomotoon, who was married to an attractive and kind girl. Before this girl had gotten married she was in love with Meromo, a young warrior of Ilmeshuki generation, but her father, Mulewo, like all Maasai parents, had total authority over her when choosing who was to be her husband. Mulewo, therefore, married his daughter to the appropriate party, Loomotoon, who had requested to marry her and had been accepted before she met Meromo. After marriage, the love of the young bride for Meromo was only intensified by the strictness of her husband, and she wanted to go back to her own chosen lover. Loomotoon, however, was known for his jealousy and constantly punished his beautiful wife in order to stop her from seeing Meromo. Although this made the young woman very scared of her husband, her fear did not stop her from running away regularly in an effort to go back to her lover. The husband—who in truth loved his wife and wanted her all to himself—went to the lover and warned him to leave his wife alone. The lover accepted the warning, but the wife still made repeated escapes to try and get him back.

One day, when the woman was about eight months pregnant, she ran away again. The husband learned of her escape soon enough to follow after her and try to bring her back. After a lengthy walk, he saw her from a distance. He walked stealthily so as not to be seen by her. When he was very close to her, the wife suddenly saw him. She was so frightened that, before her husband had even lifted a hand to hit her, she fell down and died instantly. The poor husband, heartbroken, could do nothing to save her. After performing the necessary rituals of making her body face east toward the sunrise and placing green grass on her, he left her body for vultures and other predators to dispose of.

Determined to revenge her death, the husband walked all day, until the sunset, to the lover's kraal. There he found Meromo sleeping belly-up on a bed in his mother's hut, relaxed and content. His mother, on the other bed, was very uncomfortable, however, and sensed something was wrong. By an unusual coincidence, she shouted, "Meromo, Meromo, run, my son, something is wrong" just as the woman's husband was about to cut Meromo's throat. Her son woke up in time and ran away, thwarting the husband's murderous intentions.

This case was so complex to judge that it took many years to resolve. Such matters as who should get blood cattle, how many should be paid, and who should pay them were most difficult to settle, but the Maasai never reported the case to the governmental authority because they were afraid to lose three people instead of the two who were already dead, the wife and her unborn child. After serious deliberations and repeated adjournments, the elders reached a decision. As husband of the deceased, Loomotoon could not be implicated in her death because he had every right to follow his wife and try to retrieve her. In addition, he did not actually kill her. Meromo, the lover, also could not be punished. Although he was loved by Loomotoon's wife, he had tried to discourage her and had failed. To the Maasai, love is never a

crime; nor was he ever caught actually making love with Loomotoon's wife. The parents of the girl obviously were very hurt, as any parents would be, but they could not even claim blood cattle because their girl was already married and therefore no longer belonged to them. Although many people suffered tragically in the whole affair, it had to be dismissed.

After marrying and becoming fathers, elders spend much time at their kraals looking after their children, cattle, and property. Often, the combined efforts of several families are required to cope efficiently with certain situations, security, for instance. A communal structure is essential in areas that are isolated and frequented by cattle raiders and predators. Several different families will come together to share food, labor, and, most important of all, to protect each other. Such large communities of kraals may have between ten to twenty houses, a number large enough for defense and security during attacks. The elders select a location where there is plenty of pasture and water, little wind, and level land without rocks, so the cattle can sleep comfortably. Higher places are sometimes preferred to let those at home watch the children and herds as they graze.

Families that get along well frequently build kraals together and may stay together for years, even moving with each other when grazing becomes poor and seasonal rivers dry up. The actual structure of the settlement is roughly circular. Each family builds its own houses and part of the fence enclosing the settlement. The cattle are kept in the center, and small enclosures may be built to keep sheep, goats, and calves. Each elder has his own gate to the settlement; one can easily tell the number of families living together by the number of gates. Maasai traveling are welcome in any kraal and are always greeted warmly. They need only say what age-group they belong to, and they will be directed to the house of their age-mates. Even if their age-mates are not in the kraal at the time, a place will always be found for travelers.

Their freedom as warriors being gone, elders do their best to bring up their children in the traditional Maasai manner and to prepare them to be herders or herders' wives. They teach them such things as how to remove a thorn from the hoof of a goat or sheep and how to deliver calves and lambs. They remind them constantly to love and care for cattle, as all good Maasai must. At times, an elder will hand a boy a piece of meat or some milk and then ask him whether it is sweet. When the child replies that it is, the elder urges him to love cattle because only through them can such good food be obtained. The elder teaches his children to sing songs to the cattle, such as *ewoko*, a song describing the pride of having cattle. Every day, the elder performs the many tasks of the herder. Apart from the general care and protection of the cattle, there are such other responsibilities as branding and earmarking.

Maasai elders have a strong love for their children. This affection is expressed in their many sweet names for them and in such sayings as *Melakwa aang inchu* ("As long as a man is alive, his home is never too far away"). The following story illustrates this saying:

> There was a Maasai elder who left home to go on a trip which lasted for some time. During his trip, he missed his beloved family very much. When he finally could return, he had to travel day and night for many days, for many miles, before he came close to his kraal. Near the kraal, however, there was a flooding river which was impossible to cross. Many other stranded people were waiting for the water level to drop so they might also cross. The night came and they decided to retreat and spend the night at a nearby kraal until they could try again the following day. This particular elder refused to leave, swearing that he could not stay for another day without seeing his beloved children. Despite repeated warnings, the others failed to convince him. Desperately, he plunged into the river in an effort to cross, but the force of the current pulled him downriver, and he was never seen again. While he was struggling with the water, those on the riverbank shouted to him, "Now you have made your home and children more distant than ever."

Fathers warn their children to respect anyone older, and especially elders. They tell their young ones to greet elders and respond to their greetings promptly and politely. If an elder asks a child to bring this or that thing, he or she must do it immediately, without grumbling. When an older person walks into a house and finds a child seated on a chair, the child is expected to get up and let the elder sit down as a gesture of respect. Children are taught to respect elders so as to avoid the curses they can render when they are offended. These curses are terrible— "May your own children disrespect you, my child, the way you have me." "I gave you strong hands and limbs, and I want them back." "Be barren." "Die of dysentery." Maasai society as a whole believes such curses are very effective when one deserves them, and they like to say, "What we on earth as a society accept, God above will have no choice but to accept."

Bringing up children differs from family to family.

Certain parents are strict, while others are lenient, and no one has the right to say who is right in this matter. One hears so and so is too hard on his children or so and so is too soft, his children are spoiled. Some families are strict with their children until they have been initiated into manhood or womanhood, and then they leave them alone to do what they please and decide for themselves. But others believe in the saying, *Memorataa olayoni oataa menye*, "One is never a man while his father is still alive," as is seen in the following story:

> In many parts of Africa leopards plague the herders. Tajewo's father, a shrewd individual who was known for his extraordinary love for his animals, encountered this problem many times. After one night of little sleep, a lot of shouting, and the loss of one lamb, Tajewo's father called together his five warrior sons, including Tajewo.
>
> "Fellows, if you still have ears, listen. Warriors should make a difference in this situation. With five of you here, this should stop. I am not ready to lose my animals whenever a leopard wants a meal. Starting tonight, you are going to take turns at the watch, not sleeping until the moon rises. Understand?"
>
> "Aiya," they responded in unison.
>
> "Either you kill the beast or he kills you. Let the firstborn start on the first night and run down each night to the youngest. I emphasize that there is to be no sleeping at all until the moon rises."
>
> The following two nights, the leopard did not come because he still had meat, or at least that is what the warriors thought. But one can't make that assumption because leopards are always unpredictable, even more so because they kill for the sake of killing, not only to eat.
>
> The third night the leopard came at about eight, when the warriors were still having supper. He was not expected, and no one was on guard yet. They ran to the scene when they heard the frightened flock, but the leopard was like lightning and again took another lamb. Tajewo's father was very upset, but could not blame anyone because everyone had been surprised, including himself. He punished himself by refusing to eat for two days. If Tajewo's dear father punished himself for something he did not commit, what punishment could his sons expect if one of them, his sentries, failed him? They all knew that they would wish they had never been born, because the punishment would be very severe. Tajewo's father usually punished a guilty son by

inflicting physical pain as well as giving away his cattle to a friend or relative. But in this particular case they knew that instead of the usual single cow, it would be five or six. Therefore, each of them vowed to play his part very well and to follow his father's orders.

For the next month or two, the leopard came as usual, but after discovering how alert the warriors were, he left to kill gazelles or other animals in kraals not as guarded as theirs. The sons kept careful watch for this entire time, but since the casualties were not as numerous as before, they loosened their guard. If a warrior whose sentry duty came up wanted to be with a girl, he would ask one of his brothers to take over for him, agreeing to make it up to him later. That system worked well for them. They continued with it for quite a while without being discovered by their father.

A day came when Tajewo's brother Naikosiai was to keep watch. He asked Lellia, his brother from the same mother—one who had occupied the same womb as he had—to take over for him. He wanted to be with an old girl friend he had not seen for two years who had moved to a kraal about five miles away. Lellia agreed to take Naikosiai's turn. After the usual evening's activities of gathering together, eating, and singing to the few girls who were available, Lellia departed to stand guard in the goats' den, as requested by Naikosiai. Before long, Naikosiai left for the five-mile walk to his sweetheart.

If the moon had risen, it would have been playing hide-and-seek behind scattered, windswept clouds, but it had not. The warriors in Naikosiai's kraal sang for the girls for a while, then decided to separate and sleep since they were getting tired. Lellia, at his guard, also fell asleep. They had all slept for four hours when they heard a disturbance and rushed out to listen. Before anything could be done, the cunning leopard had left with a lamb. It happened quickly. Nature had favored the leopard alone.

The loud voice of Tajewo's father, louder than anyone else's, was calling Naikosiai because he knew it was his turn at watch. Lellia responded, but his father knew it was his voice and not his brother's.

"Lellia, Lellia," his father called.
"Yes, father," responded Lellia.
"Where is Naikosiai?"
"He is here, but asleep."
"Wake him up," his father urged.
It was not long before Lellia admitted that

his brother Naikosiai wasn't there after all.

Knowing about the incident, Tajewo woke up early to tell Naikosiai what had happened so that he might find a respected elder who could ask his father for forgiveness for him. Naikosiai was about to enter the main gate when he saw Tajewo. Tajewo knew his brother got the message because his face changed and he appeared scared.

"What's the bad news?" he asked.
"Well, God has exposed you, poor fellow."
"Is that right?" Naikosiai uttered the words slowly, emphasizing the last word. His beautiful face sweated. He gazed down, at nothing in particular. He appeared disgusted, but he was more scared than annoyed. His spear and a club he was carrying supported his handsome body. He leaned on them, and said nothing for a while. When he spoke again he said, "My God." Tajewo sensed that his brother wanted to disappear from the surface of the earth. Tajewo felt sorry for him, having himself gone through such ordeals with his father many times. Before Tajewo could give his brother any advice, which might encourage him, since his mind appeared blank, Naikosiai's club dropped suddenly from his hand. Knowing he was very scared, Tajewo laughed loudly. Naikosiai joined him and they laughed hard for a long time.

Their eyes were filled with tears when they stopped. Tajewo jokingly told Naikosiai to drop his spear as well, then he would know he had surrendered. That joke made them laugh again until they had pains in their stomachs. When they recovered, they found that time was turning against them. The women had already awakened and various early morning activities were starting. They saw their father coming out of the house. Tajewo told Naikosiai to run away and consult the elder Papai, because he was highly respected by their father.

To avoid being seen by his father, Naikosiai turned and ran down the valley toward Papai's kraal. In a short time he disappeared, except for the occasional flash of light from his spear. Naikosiai met Papai, explained to him what had happened, and begged him to come to his rescue to save him from his father's all-consuming anger. Papai told him to wait until his own herd had departed for grazing and that then he could accompany him. They both left soon after and headed toward the kraal of Naikosiai's father.

Papai tried hard not to show Naikosiai his dissatisfaction with his behavior. In an attempt to lessen the tension between them, Papai commented, "Human fate is amusing at times." Naikosiai murmured in agreement and they continued to walk. When they approached the kraal they saw Naikosiai's father returning from escorting his herd to pasture. "Heifer," Naikosiai's father called out, and Papai answered "Heifer." (Traditionally, Maasai will address each other this way when one of them has given the other a heifer as a gesture of close friendship.) Naikosiai's father, knowing that Naikosiai had brought Papai with him so that he might not be punished, said to Papai, "My respect to you, Heifer, but in this case we must compromise. I am very, very upset and I intended to twice punish the fool accompanying you, but now that he has come with you to plead for forgiveness I will punish him only once."

Papai thought about this and responded, "All right, I accept, as long as I know the nature of the punishment." Naikosiai's father continued, "My first plan was to give away two of his animals to anyone who comes here requesting help, or to sell them in the market for my children's food. This first punishment I will drop now that you have come. The second punishment which I wanted to render to this unworthy child was to beat him physically, and I am going to carry that out right now with you watching." He moved toward Naikosiai, his stick raised high, and started whipping him as hard as he could. Papai told Naikosiai not to run away until his father's anger was over. "Get through it, son," he said. Over and over again, Naikosiai's father angrily lashed at his son's body. After a short time, Naikosiai started fending off the strokes with his spear and club. He thought his father was carrying this too far. As his father's anger increased, Naikosiai ran behind Papai's back and said, "Please, I have had enough, save me now." Papai intervened, "Heifer, enough, enough." Naikosiai's father stopped and stormed away from both of them, his mouth foaming and his body shaking with rage.

Papai waited until Naikosiai's father calmed down and then went to him, saying "Heifer." Barely audible, the reply came back, "Heifer." Papai continued, "Heifer, I'm sorry about all this, but you should know that children are children and not very different from ourselves at that age." Naikosiai's father replied, "I think present-day children are different from us. We were more careful and I daresay more respectful to those above ourselves in age." "Yes," Papai replied thoughtfully. "You may be right but that is life and we must live with it. Please forgive your son now that you have inflicted a few scars on his skin." Naikosiai's father responded, "Heifer, if it was anybody else who came to the rescue of this fool, I would not have given in at any cost, but you know how much I respect you, and for that reason I will forgive the fool. I give you my word of honor." Papai, now satisfied that Naikosiai was saved, left for his own kraal.

In the evening, Naikosiai's father called all of his children together, including Naikosiai, so they might hear what he had to say. He told them, "Children who do not hear and respect what their fathers say are not worth having. Any child of mine who does not respect and obey my words, like this fool here, will be outcast. My words will not be blown by the wind, you should keep that in your minds. Now you can depart, but remember, I act according to my words."

Maasai parents will sometimes pass on to their children their knowledge of traditional medicines. They place much faith in the medicinal properties of various trees, plants, and herbs to cure disease. For instance, to cure stomach pains, the bark from the cassia tree is scraped and soaked in water, and the bitter reddish liquid is given to the patient. To cure tapeworms, the bark from a species of the *albizia* tree is either boiled in water and a little milk, or chewed dry until the juice can be swallowed. For malaria, a root from the tree the Maasai call *esumeita* is ground or scraped with a knife and placed in water. The liquid is stirred until it foams and is then given to the patient, who will vomit immediately and thereby rid himself of the malarial poisons. The Maasai always try to cure an ailment or disease by themselves before they will go for outside help.

In Maasai society, there is a traditional division of labor between men and women. Women are responsible for raising children, building houses, fetching water and firewood, and milking cows. They supervise the home and prepare young girls for marriage by teaching them such necessities as sewing, beadwork, and how to take care of the young. The duties of adult men include building fence enclosures, taking care of the herds, finding and maintaining sources of water, and protecting the land. The division of tasks is generally fair, but each side tends to look down on the other's kind of work. For example, a young Maasai maiden will find it difficult or insulting to tend cattle, objecting to their kicking dust on her beautiful dress, while a Maasai boy considers it beneath him to baby-sit for his young brother or sister. The Maasai do not have institutionalized formal education. Instead, their children learn Maasai history and customs and their duties in life through observation and participation and especially through their rich oral tradition.

Women work equally as hard as men, and even harder at times. Among their most important activities is house building. First, an oblong shape the size of the house is drawn on the ground; then holes are dug and large branches inserted in them. Smaller branches are tied on top of the larger ones and are bent to conform to the desired structure of the house. The leafy parts of the branches are woven together to fill in the exposed areas. Grass is packed all around, and finally cattle dung is plastered on the sides and top to seal the structure.

The interior of the house has one room. It contains one bed, large enough for up to six people to sleep together, and one smaller and more privately situated bed for the mother of the house and her young children. The beds are made with strong branches and covered with soft hides. In the center of the house is a hearth for cooking, warmth, and light. Along the side there is usually an animal den for newborn calves or goat kids, with a barrier separating it from the rest of the house. There are no large windows, but there is an opening in either the walls or ceiling to let light in and smoke out, and the door of the house is seldom closed.

In general, Maasai women do not attend elders' meetings, except when it concerns them, and elders seldom attend women's gatherings. Anyone of either sex who attends the meetings of the other is often in an inferior position. For example, if a woman wants to make a point in an elders' meeting, she must do so while seated and not standing as elders do. That women do have authority in the society, however, is demonstrated by the *olkishuroto*. This is a gathering of women who band together and go out to punish some wrongdoing by a man. For instance, a Maasai elder may have wronged the married women of his generation by having sex with one of the daughters of his generation-mates, which is strictly forbidden. Gravely insulted by this sexual transgression, the women of the elder's generation become violent. They may slash the legs of his cattle, slaughter his favorite bull, pour cow dung over his body, and beat him severely, sometimes nearly to death. They will also give a serious beating to the woman involved and pour cow dung over her head as well. Another reason for an *olkishuroto* might be if an elder tried to prevent a woman from fulfilling one of her religious duties.

Others who commit sex-oriented crimes, such as warriors who sleep with women of their father's generation, are punished by the elders. Having sex with any married woman outside of one's own

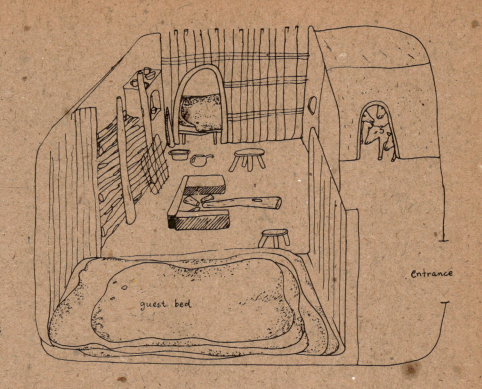

Interior and ground plan of Maasai dwellings

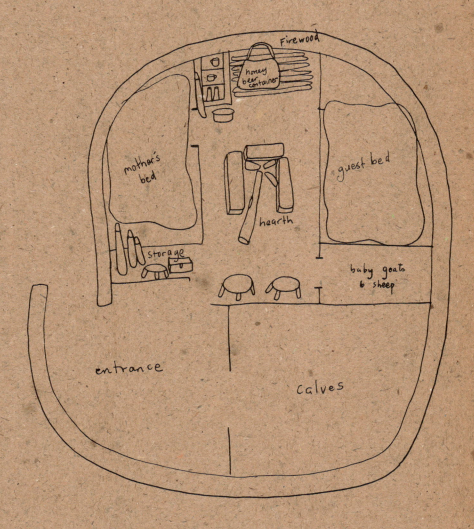

generation is a crime, but making love to a woman married to a generation-mate of one's father is additionally regarded as incest. This is because all of the women in the generation of a man's father are considered to be his mother. The punishments for this crime may include exposure to the community's anger, a fine of a heifer, or refusal of marriage to a daughter of that generation. Elders will say, "One cannot make love to a mother and marry her daughter."

Whenever many Maasai women get together, they sing and dance among themselves. Beautifully adorned with multicolored bead necklaces and long, soft, lamb-hide dresses, they offer prayer songs thanking God for His blessings or asking Him to bring them children, rain, grass, prosperity, and peace. Women in Maasailand pray to God more often than men do. As part of their prayer ritual, they sprinkle milk in three directions, the North, South, and East (the West, where the sun sets, is used only for cursing). They will murmur in a small, very humble voice:

> *Enjoo iyook engeraa.*
> Give us children.
> *Injoo iyook ingishu.*
> Give us cattle.
> *Iye akekisilig.*
> Our hope is with you always.

Women often gather in large prayer meetings, called *Alamal Loonkituak,* which are very emotional and exceedingly sentimental. All men, and particularly elders, are scared of the power of these meetings. Men may not do anything that might tamper with the meetings, but rather must supply all the things necessary for them, such as animals for sacrifices. Most of these large congregations gather to pray for children, to visit special holy places like Mount Lengai or special holy trees, where the Maasai offer such sacrifices as lambs without spots. Whenever a Maasai passes by a holy tree, he or she will pluck green grass, put it on the tree, and then pray. Sometimes bead necklaces, bracelets, or anklets are placed on the tree as well.

Women also pray for barren women, as in the following prayer, offered by a group of women:

> *Naai, irukoki iyiook*
> O God, grant to us
> *Nena nikiomonito iyie.*
> The things that we pray for.
> *Inchoo olgos olala osho,*
> Grant her the joy of motherhood,
> *Entito aasho olayoni.*

> Let her bear and cherish.
> *Inchoo metoisho nerik,*
> God, give her a shade to rest under,
> *Naai, injoo oloip lemeolalchani.*
> But not the one of a tree.

A more personal prayer song of a barren woman:

> *Adung'ito ilpurkeli maariko,*
> I cross savannahs unescorted,
> *Naipuroki ilng'atunyo.*
> And the lion roars at me.
> *Naipuroki olowaru oju,*
> The black-maned lion roars at me,
> *Naipuroki olemeju,*
> And the one without a mane.
> *Naipuroki olowaru oju*
> The black-maned lion alongside the zebra.
> *Obotere iloitikoshi.*
> I pray to the One with many colors
> *Aamon olasira ingumoki peeaisho.*
> So He will give me a child.
> *Kitoni olmasi onyil laelie*
> Then I can stay home like a
> *Esekekwa engerai.*
> Real woman and stop wandering.

This song tells how lonely a Maasai woman without a child can be. She has to travel frequently to holy places to pray, and sometimes must go alone. She may encounter many dangers on her frequent visits to the *Laibon,* whom she begs to help her with medicines or charms so she can bear a child. A Maasai woman without a child is often very unhappy, and people sympathize with her. Although adoption of children is sometimes possible in Maasailand, a woman is not fully happy until she conceives one herself.

The laws of inheritance are an important feature of Maasai family life. While still young, each Maasai child, male or female, is given a cow, a ewe, and a female goat. These animals are known as *ingishu emisigiyoyi,* birthright cattle, and if the child is lucky they multiply as he or she grows up. By the time of elderhood, a Maasai usually has a good herd.

When a girl gets married, she does not take her personal herd with her, but leaves them with her brothers or, if she has none, with her mother. If she is ever in need, she may go to them and ask for a cow or two; and the request is usually granted. When the girl goes to her new husband's home, she is given cattle by her husband and his relatives to form a new herd of her own. Both husband and wife now have their own herds, but the husband has control over his wife's.

When a junior elder marries and has performed all the ceremonies required to attain full elderhood, he may leave his father's home with his wife and children and build his own kraal if he so desires. Others continue to stay with their own fathers, but they assume control of their own wealth of cattle. It becomes difficult for a man to have his father controlling his wealth when he himself is a father. A Maasai who tries to supervise his older son's movements or wealth always encounters difficulties, and if he persists, the son will report the matter to the community elders who have the authority to allow him to leave and build his own kraal like other elders.

When the father of a family dies, his eldest son inherits all his personal cattle; when the mother dies, the youngest son inherits all of hers. The middle sons acquire the cattle belonging to their sisters who do not take their cattle with them when they marry and go to their new husband's home. If a man dies childless, or leaves daughters only, his brothers inherit his cattle. If a man dies and leaves a son who is still young, the property the son inherits is taken care of for him until he grows up.

Maasai elders observe the sky daily. By looking at the movement of the stars, they can tell when it is about to rain. Experts in the solar calendar, the elders have divided the month into thirty days according to the position of the moon, and they believe it is important to observe the changes in the moon carefully. Lunar shape, color, and position determine the timing of certain crucial activities in Maasailand. For instance, the Maasai prefer to attack their enemies during the full moon, when the moon appears slightly red in color. When the moon is full and white in color, the Maasai choose to hold their major ceremonies. When the moon dies, or disappears, the Maasai will not undertake any major work or ceremony. Even moving from one place to another is prohibited at such times. To the Maasai, the disappearance of the moon symbolizes death, and they try to avoid the bad luck that might befall them during that time.

When a person dies among the Maasai, the relatives weep a great deal. They anoint the body with lamb or ox fat and make new sandals for the deceased to speed his or her onward journey. A cattle stick is put in the hand of a man to symbolize his work as a herder. Similarly, for a woman, such tools of her trade as a sewing needle or a calabash are placed at her side. The left arm is folded to support the head, and the body is placed facing east toward the sunrise. The body is left out in the open to be cleared away by wild animals. In case the beasts do not discover the body, a sheep is slaughtered and its fat roasted near the body.

The strong aroma of the meat will always attract the beasts to clear the body away. The deceased person's name will never be mentioned again by the family. Should there be anyone or anything that is called by the deceased's name, it is given another name which is not like that of the deceased.

Circumstances are somewhat different upon the death of an elder with children. His name continues to be spoken since his descendants are named after him. The last rituals for a family man also are different. A bullock is slaughtered, and the corpse is anointed with its fat. All the meat of the bullock is eaten on the spot. After new sandals are made, the corpse is carried out to a shady place and left so that the hyenas may smell it and come and carry it away. If the predators fail to clear away the body, a sheep is slaughtered and its meat and bones are left beside the corpse to attract scavengers. When the father of a family dies, the whole family mourns for him. His wives and daughters must remove their ornaments, necklaces, and earrings. His sons, both youths and warriors, will shave their heads, as they also do whenever a warrior brother or close relative dies. The mourning usually lasts for one month. When a woman or child dies, she is mourned, but the members of her family do not remove their ornaments nor shave their heads.

On the death of a *Laibon* or a rich person, the corpse is not left out in the open. An ox or sheep is slaughtered, and fat is taken and rubbed on the body. Then the body is put on an oxhide and carried to a shady spot. A grave is dug, and the body is placed in it. After the grave is covered, stones in a pyramid shape are piled upon it. Whenever people pass the grave, they throw stones onto the heap as a sign of respect. This is done for all time.

The Maasai believe that, upon death, the souls of important men turn into snakes and reappear on earth. Sometimes, when an important man has recently died, a snake is seen by his family in an unusual circumstance, such as on the chair where he used to sit or by the waterhole where his cattle used to drink. In ordinary circumstances, the Maasai would kill such a snake, but in this case they never do so, but rather try to feed it milk until it goes away by itself.

Meeta olmoruo orngiro means "There is no frail elder; all elders deserve respect." What will be the future of Maasai elders? Will they continue to command the respect they have enjoyed traditionally, now that Maasailand is changing? Will their wisdom be as fully utilized as it is presently? The answers are by no means clear.

Elderhood marks
a period of responsibility for men and women,
beginning with marriage, the building of a family,
and the acquisition of wealth and security in the form of
children and cattle. But numerous social occasions,
ceremonies, and rituals also fill their lives. The able and
gregarious woman is particularly singled out for
praise, just as the wise and judicious man earns the
respect of his peers. At group ceremonies, women and
men arrive separately, usually in a stately and joyous
procession, and greet one another with elaborate and
formal courtesies. Admired and treated with
deference by all younger persons, the Maasai elder looks
forward to an old age not of isolation and fear but
of continuing involvement in
the life of the people.

One of the first concerns of new elders, as well as of recently circumcised girls, is marriage. Although the match may have been arranged long in advance, there is much excitement as the wedding day approaches. The best man (*above*) and the bride's family are ochered, shaved, and dressed in finery. Necklaces are polished; beautiful beaded skins are prepared for the bride.

Following page, right, the bride is lovingly dressed by her mother in the softest skins. *Left*, the bride and groom are then ready to depart from her *engang* to go and live together in his. The bride traditionally shows much sorrow in leaving her home, and she is forbidden to look back, for fear that she might turn to stone from grief.

199

As the bride leaves her family *engang* escorted by the
women of her family, she is blessed by her father with
milk from a calabash. The groom and his best man lead
her to her new home, the best man removing any
obstacles in her path. As she goes, carrying a white
walking stick, she proceeds slowly, looking downward.

As the wedding party reaches its destination—the
groom's *engang*—the groom and best man are greeted by
children who bow their heads respectfully. After the
bride enters her new home, wedding guests bring gifts
of milk. Meat and honey beer are consumed, and
joyous singing and dancing celebrate the bond.

One of the first responsibilities of a newly married
woman is to build her home. The basic structure is
formed by weaving long tree branches together. Open
spaces are patched with leaves and grass before a final
coating of dung is plastered over the entire surface.

Women are creative in making their homes. Though
all houses conform to a basic shape, the women may
vary the entrances, decorate the exteriors with symbolic
markings, or modify details of the interior—the hearth,
sleeping quarters, and animal pen. Maintaining the
house, and especially keeping it weather tight, are also
the woman's responsibilities. Just before the rainy season
she will patch the roof, filling the cracks with fresh dung.

As cattle people, the Maasai rely on milk as their main food. It is drunk both fresh and in a sour form, as yogurt. Women milk the cows twice a day—in the morning before they leave for pasture and in the evening after their return. Children may assist in milking goats and also help the adults *(above)* in encouraging those baby goats who may not be getting enough to drink to nurse from the she-goats with the most milk. After milking, the small animals are led into the *engang* and bedded down in the family pens.

Calabashes for collecting and storing milk and honey beer are made from gourds, which are cut from their vines, dried, scooped out inside, and decorated with beads, cowries, and a leather strap.

After a calabash is used, it is washed out with water and then sterilized with burning embers from the wild olive tree. The embers, which impart a smoky flavor to the milk, are removed with two long sticks, one for scrubbing the sides and another, with a cow's-tail brush, to clean out all the remaining charcoal.

In addition to milking the cows, building and maintaining the houses, and preparing the calabashes, the women also regularly collect water and firewood.

212

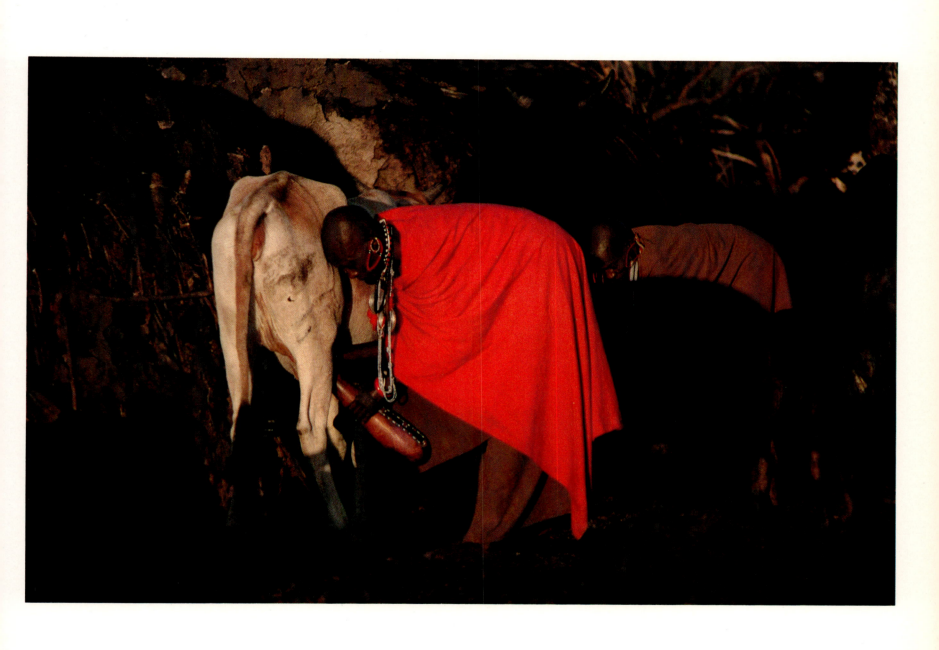

Maasai women take special care with their personal
ornamentation—beadwork in particular—and with their
clothing, made both of cloth and hides. Preparing animal
skins by scraping and stretching them, they soften and
color the hides with ocher and animal fat and add
beads for decoration. Ropes are made from leather by
cutting narrow strips and pulling them into long lengths.
Cloth garments of white factory-made textiles are dyed
in ocher; when mothers shake out the freshly dipped
ochered clothes to remove excess moisture, children
often dash beneath to get some fresh color on their own
clothing. After chores, women gather to bead necklaces
and other ornaments.

The major ceremony marking the full confirmation of
elderhood is called *Olngesherr,* when all the men who
were warriors together are reunited and given one
generation-name. A large ceremonial manyatta is
constructed, and at its center is placed the symbol of the
ceremony *(above),* a mound of cow dung containing a
stone from a special stream and a long branch from a
sacred tree.

Elders arrive at the manyatta months in advance, each
bringing a favorite wife and selected cattle. Their leaders
wear special togas of decorated hides; those who are
known to be the most generous and honest are honored
by having their forearms wrapped with blue beads.

During the months of preparation for *Olngesherr*, ceremonial visits to the ritual manyatta are paid by elders from other parts of Maasailand. For these visits, called *Alamal*, both men and women adorn themselves with their finest jewelry and new clothing. In addition to ocher, a special blue makeup is used by some Maasai.

The visitors at *Alamal* arrive in long processional lines, singing and carrying white walking sticks. After elaborate formal greetings, the men retire to feasting places in the bush, and the women are given parts of the slaughtered animals to prepare in their houses. Following the feasting, all the guests gather to sing, dance, and drink honey beer late into the night.

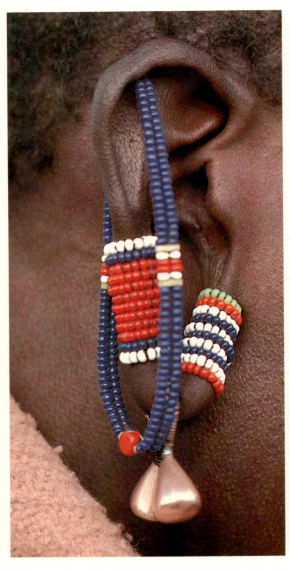
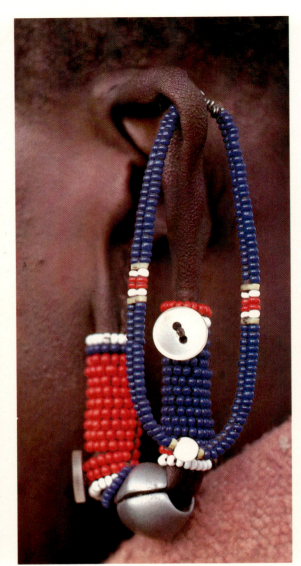

The white sticks that the dancing junior elders carry here are symbols of peace.

Olngesherr begins on a day, usually near full moon, designated by the *Laibon.* Prior to the ceremony, an unblemished bull has been selected—one either totally black or white or with a light patch on its chest and not having spots or broken horns. The bull is captured at dawn by the elders and suffocated at the center of the manyatta. Its dewlap is slit, and blood is forced out by puncturing its heart. A powdered charm from the *Laibon* is dusted into the liquid. One by one, starting with the owner of the beast and then the two generation-chiefs, the hundreds of new elders kneel and drink. As the blood diminishes, milk or honey beer is added to give each participant a full measure of the ritual drink.

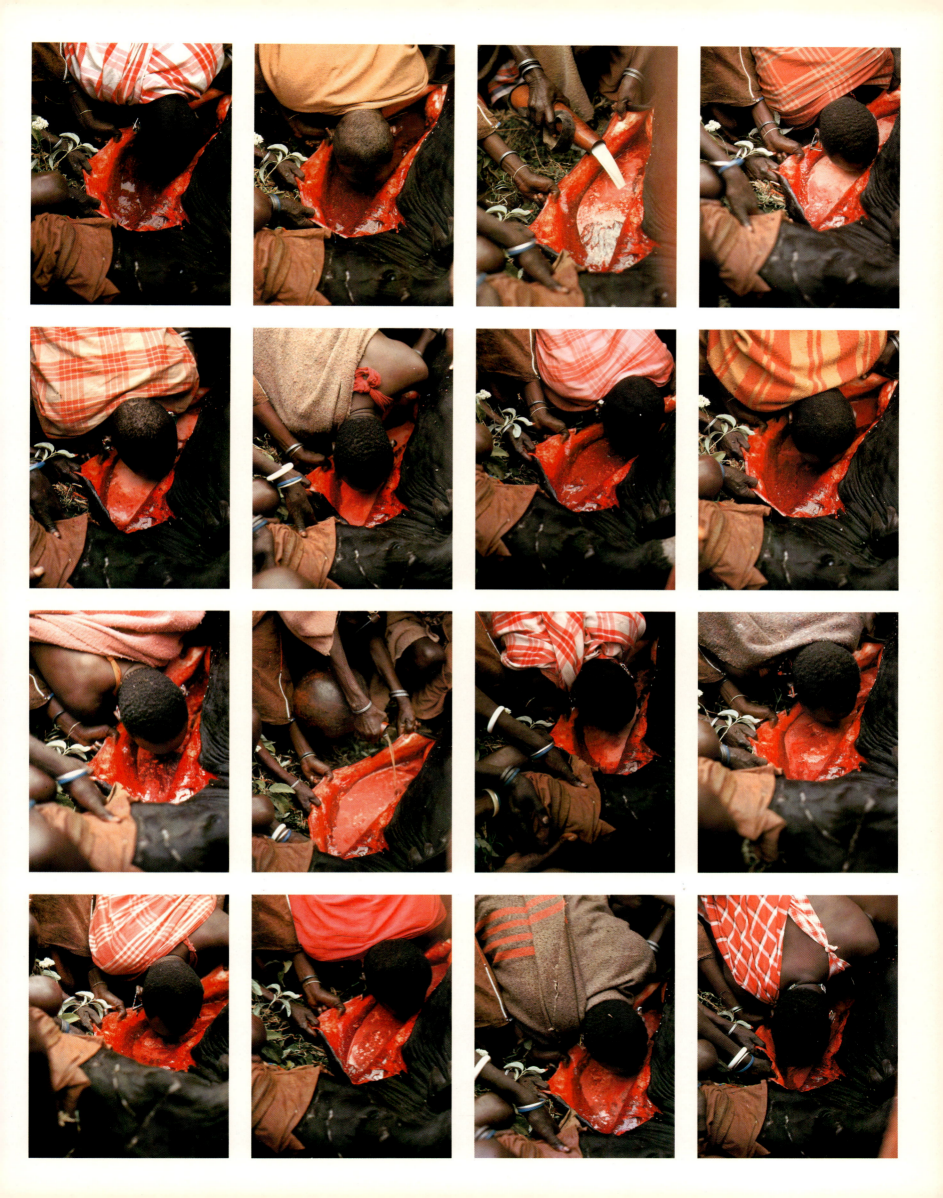

The wives erect a large enclosure where the ox was killed, and here, over the next two days, all rituals will occur.

After the enclosure has been constructed, the senior elders supervise the butchering and roasting of the sacrificial ox within it. All the new initiates gather inside, and the senior elders then bless each new junior elder by rubbing a piece of fatty chest meat on his forehead and giving him a bite of the meat.

The following morning, the new elders assemble again for a milk blessing, since meat and milk may not be taken together. Each is given a drink of sour milk from a large gourd and then receives a finger-ring made from the underbelly of the bull slaughtered the day before. Later, the senior elders smear the chalky paint called *enturoto* on the faces of the initiates.

An important part of the *Olngesherr* ceremony is the ritual blessing of the new elders' cattle sticks, in the following manner. Simultaneously with the blessings just mentioned, the senior elders oversee the heating of the initiates' branding irons. When they have become red hot, these irons are plunged into a pool of cow urine, which has been gathered previously by the women. The new junior elders then dash excitedly to the pool to bless their cattle sticks by waving them through the steaming vapor that rises.

Afterwards, each new junior elder collects his personal branding irons from the pool. He will use them to mark his herds with his own distinctive brand.

The new elders are blessed with these words: "May you be peaceful and prosperous, with many cattle and children."

Toward the end of the final day of *Olngesherr*, the skin of the ceremonial bull is stretched out to dry by the women. Each woman may hammer in two stakes if she has not dishonored herself by having sexual relations with a warrior below her husband's generation. After the skin dries, a special mark of three parallel straight lines is made on the hairy side.

As the final blessing of *Olngesherr*, one of the most revered of the senior elders circles the manyatta and plants a shoot of green grass at the cattle entrance of the house of each new elder. He anoints it with honey beer, whispering a blessing for the future of each new elder.

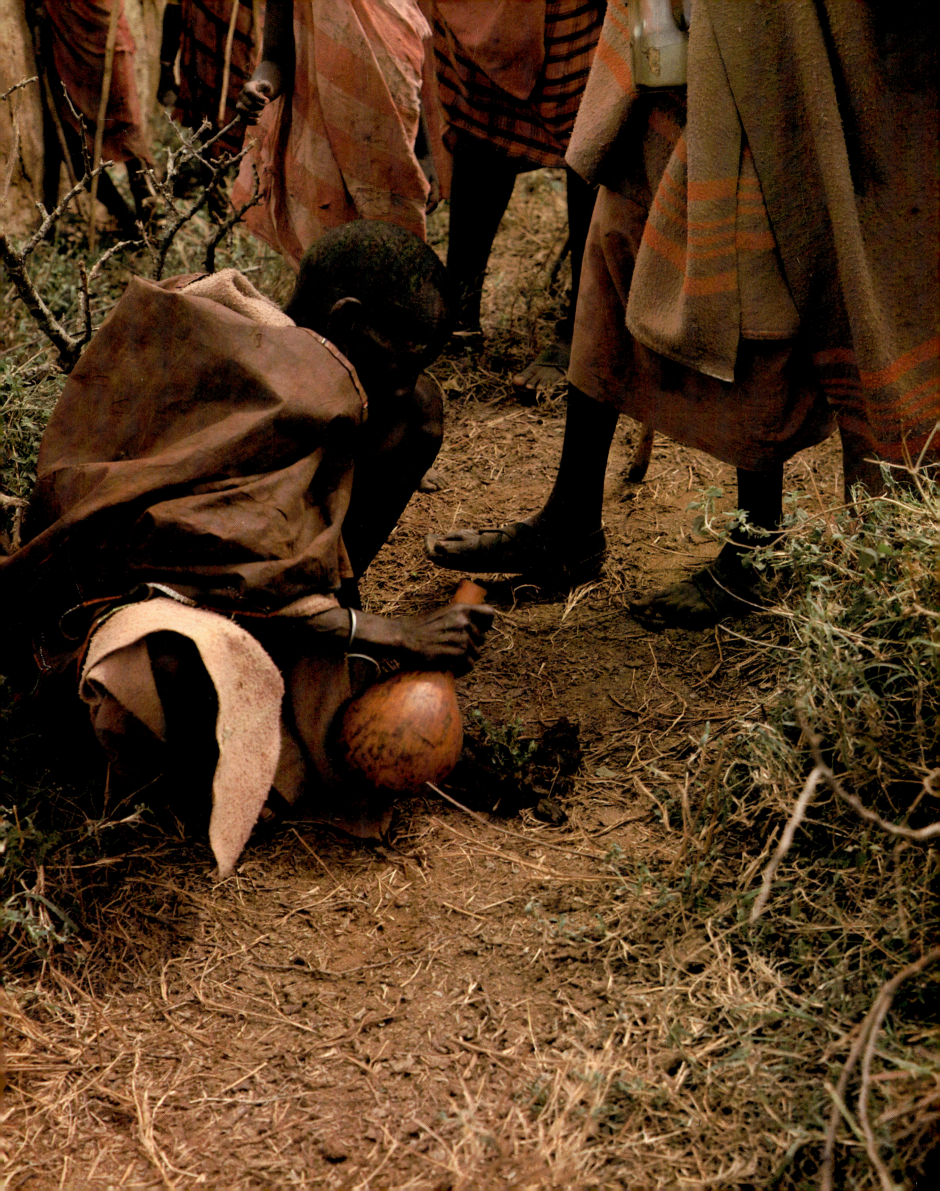

Maasai elders protect their herds from predators and natural accidents (such as those incurred when bulls fight for dominance of the herd), keep them in good health, and assure their procreation.

Elders often assist at times of calving, especially at a
difficult delivery. In this sequence of pictures, a calf is
pulled from its mother and then, having shown weak
signs of life, it is given mouth-to-mouth resuscitation.

    Since the animals of many different families may graze
together, elders take particular care to brand and mark
them for identification. Brands on the flanks and
foreheads, in addition to slits or notches in the ears,
serve to mark an animal's ownership by clan, family, and
individual. A large and unusually fine herd of cattle may
include an animal with distinctive branded decorations
covering its entire body. Long and beautifully curved horns
are prized by all.

251

At the *Olkiteng Lorrbaa* ceremony, male and female junior elders play at fighting, using branches and competing for a skewer of meat.

255

The dignified state of senior elderhood brings about
a natural retirement from some activities but also an
increased sense of community affairs. Elders become
more sedentary in their ways and reflective in their
bearing. They acquire a traditional look that includes a
warm blanket worn as a cloak, the carrying of a fly
whisk made of wildebeeste tail hair, a walking staff, and,
for special occasions, a beaded calfskin cloak. Many also
carry a beaded bamboo tobacco container, which they
may wear around their necks; these are always presented
to them by their first-born daughters. As elders gather to
talk in the evenings, to tell stories and discuss important
issues, they preserve Maasai legend and lore.

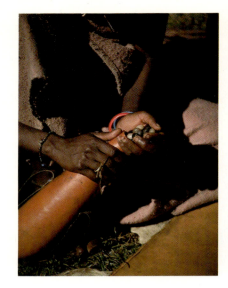
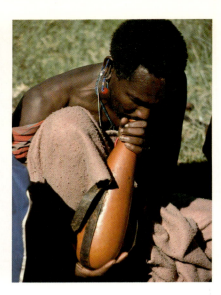

The most feared and respected elder is the *Laibon,* who combines qualities of spiritual leader, diviner, rituals expert, and healer. Pictured here is the famous *Laibon* Simel of Kenya, wearing a cloak made from the fur of the rare tree hyrax for this formal portrait. *Above,* the *Laibon* supervises his sons as they cast a prophecy by a procedure called *engidong.* Smooth river stones are placed in a calabash; the diviner whispers and spits into the calabash, beseeching his great ancestors, Mbatian and Nelion, to aid him. He then pours out the stones, counting them out into small piles. Repeating the process a number of times, he will eventually make a prophecy or answer a question posed to him.

Elders spend much of their time in quiet pursuits. *Above,* an elder cannily scrutinizes the moves of a young warrior playing the game of *engehei,* variants of which are known all over Africa. In Maasailand, the game is played on a "board" of from six to sixteen pairs of depressions carved in wood or stone or even dug in the earth. The game's challenge is to anticipate the movement and distribution of pieces, blocking and capturing the greatest number. *Opposite,* two old friends chat, another prepares a chew of tobacco, and an elder whose daughter is about to be

initiated has his head shaved by his wife.

Elders gather for more serious discussions in a special council called *olkiama*. There, questions of inheritance, murder, divorce, or theft are discussed in open forum. Each elder has his say. Although eloquence is respected, resolution occurs only when a clear consensus is reached; no vote is taken. Wrongdoers are never imprisoned, but instead punishment or recompense is meted out as fines of cattle. Maasai justice is fair, humane, and eminently practical.

A Personal Reflection

From the farm, the tragic fate of the disappearing Masai tribe on the other side of the river could be followed from year to year. They were fighters who had been stopped fighting, a dying lion with his claws clipped, a castrated nation. Their spears had been taken from them, their big dashing shields even, and in the Game Reserve the lions followed their herds of cattle.

Isak Dinesen, *Out of Africa*

The readers of this book may want to know what the future holds for the Maasai. As a Maasai who sympathizes with my people and culture, I may sound pessimistic, but I have reason to be. The Maasai are a people whose time has passed. The industrialized world is closing in upon them like a flood out of control, and they must move to higher ground to save themselves.

After deep reflection on my people and culture, I have painfully come to accept that the Maasai must change to protect themselves, if not their culture. They must adapt to the realities of the modern world and become part of it for the sake of their own survival. It is better to meet an enemy out in the open and to be prepared for him than for him to come upon you at home unawares. The Maasai do not yet have all the weapons necessary to confront the modern world.

They must have education, land, and resources to enable them to fit into a money economy. As of now, the Maasai have cattle and land for their sustenance, but they are losing their land at a frightening rate. If their land goes, there will be no place to graze cattle, and the Maasai way of life will die.

The Maasai's biggest problem today is this loss of their land. The problem goes as far back as the early 1900s, when the Maasai, owning so much land, came into conflict with European settlers. The colonial governments encouraged settlers coming from England and South Africa to move into Maasailand, and they paid no compensation to the Maasai. When the Maasai resisted this colonization, they made enemies of the colonial authority. In addition, the colonial authority saw the well-organized Maasai warriors as a potential threat and therefore felt doubly uneasy.

In June, 1901, Sir Charles Eliot, the colonial governor of Kenya and a staunch supporter of the settlers, wrote, "I regard the Maasai as the most important and dangerous of the tribes with whom we have to deal in East Africa and I think it will be long necessary to maintain an adequate military force in the district which they inhabit." The attitude of the British government toward the Maasai was one of suspicion and uncertainty. A subcommissioner in the Ukamba

At left:
In dignified old age stands the father of the
author, Lemeikoki Ole Ngiyaa.

province of Kenya, by the name of Ainsworth, also wrote, "A policy of gradually bringing these people under our control is better than one of using absolute force at once. . . . After a time, when our military forces are more organized and our Administration is more extended, we shall be more able to edge the nomad tribes, and by degrees make it impossible to wander about without our permission. We could clearly define the Maasai lands and see that the limits were kept."

By 1910, Eliot had succeeded in evicting the Maasai from the fertile Laikipia highlands in favor of the settlers, led by Lord Delamere. The Maasai were moved from Laikipia despite the fact that the colonial secretary in London had ordered the move to stop. Charles Eliot was subsequently forced to resign thanks to the efforts of Ole Gilisho, a Maasai leader, the sympathetic Dr. Norman Leys (who was expelled from Kenya because of this), and other Maasai leaders, who defended their position in a letter to the colonial secretary and in the courts. However, the land taken by the settlers was never returned to the Maasai, not even after Kenya achieved independence in 1963.

A series of Land Acts passed by the Kenyan government after independence formally opened Maasailand to land buyers. The Maasai found it difficult to believe that land, which belonged to God, could be sold as a commodity. Vulnerable and ignorant of their rights in this land issue, they were taken advantage of by the land buyers. Since land was communally owned by the Maasai, a land buyer could acquire parcels without the consent of all the owners by bribing or forging a land title in the name of one owner. Additionally, the Maasai owner would often be unaware of the meaning and formalities of a land title, and his thumbprint signature was often obtained by devious means by the buyer. Much land belonging to the Maasai was taken in this way.

In Tanzania the land situation was a bit different. Tanzania was first colonized by Germans, who were more interested in administration than settlement. Soon after the Germans were defeated in World War I, the British administration replaced them and governed the country not as a colony, like Kenya, but as a trusteeship under the League of Nations. A few settlers were brought in to occupy the area between Mount Kilimanjaro and Mount Meru called Engare Nanyuki, which is the part of Maasailand bordering lands of the Meru tribe. The settlers came into conflict with the local peoples, who eventually took their complaints to the United Nations. The United Nations sent a delegation to the area to study the land issue. The delegation recommended independence for the nation, but did not resolve the land problem. When independence came, the disputed land was never given back to the Maasai but was instead taken over by the government.

As time went on, more land was taken for public use, mainly for national parks. To exacerbate the problem, certain non-Maasai Africans engaged in agriculture started encroaching upon Maasailand, and nothing was done to stop them. In Tanzania today, all the land belongs to the government and is open to every individual to exploit. Those tribes which were land-hungry, like the Wa-Arusha (the agricultural Maasai), WaMeru, and WaChaga, took advantage of the situation, and the pastoral Maasai felt the pinch. As more land is taken away from the Maasai, they will be forced to move their herds illegally into the game parks, and this in turn will further deplete the wild animals and park lands by overburdening grazing lands, water supplies, and other resources.

The Serengeti wild animal herds are still thundering across the savannahs of Maasailand, but their days are numbered, as are those of the Maasai culture. As fate will have it, the people and the herds will either die together, or flourish, if protected and cared for. Maasailand, for the first time, is becoming crowded, and not because the Maasai birthrate has increased dramatically—in truth, it has not, for the infant mortality rate is still very high and proper medical care is still largely absent. The overcrowding in Maasailand is the result of external encroachment by farmers, who need the same kind of areas for their agriculture as the Maasai do for their herds, usually highlands with permanent waterholes and potential for dry-season grazing. Such encroachment is forcing the Maasai to gamble with semiarid areas, which are only suitable for grazing during the rainy season and cannot withstand excessive use. Overuse of such areas has led to deterioration of the environment as well as loss of domestic and wild animals.

To get the maximum profit from the land, the government of Kenya has introduced a process of land adjudication opening Maasailand to external forces through land titles or "range schemes." These are radical moves, never known in the area before. Other tribes that understand the importance of land are now able to buy land in Maasailand, and the few Maasai who have an education know how to get title deeds to monopolize large tracts of land for themselves in better areas, a thing most uninformed Maasai came to take note of too late. "Range schemes"—parcels of land owned by a group of people and used either for growing wheat or raising cattle—are now a common sight all over Kenyan Maasailand, even in the most arid places. This radical move has dislodged many Maasai. It has forced many of them to come to Nairobi and other cities looking for the only jobs they can do, such as security guards. The great bravery and trustworthiness for which the Maasai are known enable them to secure these jobs. Standing sentry all night while others are sleeping is now the fate of the noble Maasai.

Before the Kenya Parliamentary Land Acts were passed for the benefit of the nation, the Maasai had two things, land and cattle, even though they had no education. They were able to feed themselves and retain their cultural pride. The loss of their land seemed to shatter everything. Soon their cattle will be gone; their sustenance and culture will follow suit. When this protective umbrella is removed for good, the Maasai will flood into Nairobi and other cities, as other tribes once did. They will work not only as security guards but at any job available, and if they fail to get jobs, they will create shanty towns that will lead to crime.

In the past, the colonial authority ignored the education of the Maasai. It viewed the Maasai romantically, with the "noble savage" attitude. It did very little to help the Maasai to change, being afraid that the Maasai would not accept a position of servitude. The Maasai were not included, therefore, in the colonial program of educating native Africans to fill white-collar or clerical positions. Other tribes took advantage of this program, although the better positions were reserved for whites. This attitude of benign neglect toward the Maasai continued until independence.

During colonial times, there were very few schools in Maasailand and the few that existed were run by missionaries and were largely filled with non-Maasai children. After primary school, the Maasai schoolchildren mostly went back home to become warriors. In general, the colonial authority, which knew the importance of education, did not want to educate the Maasai, and the Maasai for their part understood neither the value of Western education nor the inevitable changes to come. They were satisfied to be left alone, their culture intact, supported with a good wealth of cattle. On occasion, however, the Maasai were forced to deal with the reality of colonial authority. Aside from the whole matter of land appropriation, the difference between the Maasai and the European concepts of justice made settlement of disputes difficult. A true story, which occurred relatively recently, illustrates well the bitter lack of understanding between the two cultures:

The Maasai call the year 1946 *Olari Otarieki Olmusungui*, "The year a European was killed." Scores of Maasai born in that year identify themselves with the phrase. Those were the years when the British authorities resorted to fining the Maasai severely for cattle raiding. They would confiscate Maasai cattle rather than imprison the Maasai because they found that many of them died while in jail. With their ideal of freedom, the Maasai resented imprisonment and human humiliation and accepted death more willingly. Many of them died in prison at that time, their fragile temperament like that of American Indians when faced with white men's jails.

This particular case concerns a Maasai warrior of the Ingidongi clan, the Maasai *Laibon* family, who went on a cattle raid and was caught and fined. While in a slaughtering camp, he got word from the colonial authority through an intermediary that nine of his cattle would be confiscated. He accepted the fine and informed the emissary to tell the District Commissioner to take the cattle—and, if necessary, the whole herd—except for one bullock which he especially loved. The commissioner thought the man arrogant and wanted to show that he himself was even more so. He went ahead and took the nine cattle, and among them was the forbidden bull. The warrior was told of the news in his retreat. With very few words he left the camp early and went to the Loita market in Kenya. There he found many cattle buyers, including the District Commissioner, who was supervising the cattle sales. Among the cattle in the ring were the warrior's fine animals and his war bull, who was trying to find an exit but could not. Without a word, the warrior speared the District Commissioner, killing him instantly.

Amid scampering and running people, the warrior removed his spear and used the European's hair to clean the bloodstains from it. People were running in all directions for their lives, sellers and buyers leaving their money and other articles, and in a matter of minutes the crowded marketplace turned into a ghost town. All the Maasai in the crowd had disappeared, except for one man, the brother of the warrior. He followed his brother, who was walking across the market with his spear pointed forward as if ready to insert it once again into another person. The warrior was like a cornered animal, but turned back abruptly when he heard his brother call his name. His brother asked him where he was going after such a crime, and the warrior replied calmly, "Where can I go when I don't know where the authority is? They seem to have run away, all of them." "Come along with me," his brother commanded. Following without a protest, the warrior was handed over to the authority. After a court case he was hanged and all his cattle, which were many, were confiscated.

As a whole, the Maasai were never happy with the judgment of the case. They thought the District Commissioner deserved his fate, because he should have respected the pride of the Maasai warrior and should not have taken the one bull the warrior asked to keep. If necessary, he could have taken the whole herd of cattle, as the Maasai himself had suggested, but not the forbidden one.

While the present governments' attitude toward the Maasai is different from that of the colonial governments, they have yet to demonstrate by action that they want to help the Maasai catch up with the rest of the people of Kenya and Tanzania. It is a lamentable fact that major needs like education, health care, water availability, and veterinary care are still very much neglected. It is the responsibility of the new African governments to win the trust of their people by being sensitive and responsive to their needs. After Tanzanian independence in 1961, the new government tried to force the Maasai to change their traditional way of dressing to the European way. Such negative acts of coercion do not bring development but, rather, alienate the people.

The governments of Kenya and Tanzania, it seems, do not want to accept the fact that they do not understand people who still live in traditional ways. They think they know what is good for these people without even asking them how they feel or what they want for their own development. And the traditional people have always viewed the government as a threat to them rather than as a force they can use to help them. For example, the Maasai were accustomed to seeing government agents only when they would appear to collect taxes, a thing which the Maasai never saw the benefit of. Traditional people developed a distrust and misunderstanding of government motives and an unwillingness to cooperate.

The government could help traditional people by approaching them with a desire to understand them rather than with threatening demonstrations of power. One major way for the government to help is to educate the Maasai in their localities to work among their own people and to win their trust in order to make the necessary transition into the twentieth century. They could try to convince the Maasai with reason and patience to accept education for their own survival. Educated Maasai could work closely with the elders to define clearly the problems confronting their areas and present them to the government.

As for the Maasai land that has been turned into national parks, the income gained from tourism there should be channeled back to develop the Maasai. Many bad development ideas adopted during the time of the colonial governments have been continued by the new independent African governments in the 1960s. One such is a preference for agriculture over cattle. The governments should accept that cattle themselves are assets of great value and that, therefore, agriculture should not be allowed to encroach on grazing lands. Efforts should be made to improve the quality of Maasai stocks as a source of milk and protein for the whole country.

The Maasai should also be helped to participate in a money economy as contributors and not as beggars. This can only be done if the governments ensure that the resources derived from Maasailand should benefit the Maasai people first and foremost.

Those few educated Maasai should live up to one purpose—to help the masses of Maasai catch up with the rest of modern Kenya and Tanzania. We may differ in how we approach the development of our people, but those differences should not divert us from the common desire which we all share. This desire is to see our people live and prosper. I will conclude by saying one thing more.

Our ancestors led our people beyond their farthest horizons. Their strength and might may be seen in our legends as well as in the size of our land. With their gleaming spearpoints and broad shields, they acquired the best grazing land in East Africa, the pride of any herder. They played their parts well, and we are proud of them for it. If this noble race of men must now be humble and destitute because of the passage of time, we do not have to accept disgrace and the disappearance of our race. We must adapt to new situations in order to survive. I do not underestimate the challenges ahead, but we must stand up to them in the way we conquered Endikir Ekerio, our legendary escarpment, and the many famines and wars of the past. Our spearpoints are now like the teeth of infants, and it seems the wisdom of the elders no longer counts, but we must survive. We must not follow the way of those races of men who have vanished from the surface of the earth. We have our culture and our governments behind us and our courage, pride, and noble truth. All we need now is determination, and jointly with all other African peoples we will not only survive but multiply and prosper.

ACKNOWLEDGMENTS

We acknowledge our gratitude to all those who have helped us in one way or another in creating this book. Special mention must go to James Ole Sekerot, C.C.M. Secretary, Monduli, Tanzania; Amos Meshuko Ole Pello; Captain Bob Nasser; Sandra Soprani; Moiyo Ole Keiwua; and to both of our parents—Lemeikoki Ole Ngiyaa, and his ever helpful family, and Betty and Leo Beckwith—for their support and encouragement.

The following published works have been of particular help in researching the text:

Hollis, (Sir Alfred) Claude. *The Maasai, Their Language and Folklore*. Oxford: Clarendon Press, 1905.

Matthiessen, Peter, and Porter, Eliot. *The Tree Where Man Was Born: The African Experience*. New York: Avon Press, 1974.

Mol, Fr. Frans. *Maa. A Dictionary of the Maasai Language and Folklore: English—Maasai*. Nairobi: Marketing and Publishing, Ltd., 1978.

Salvadori, Cynthia, and Fedders, Andrew. *Maasai*. London: Collins, 1973.

Sankan, S. S. *The Maasai*. Nairobi: East African Literature Bureau, 1971.

Waldock, Jill. *People of the World—The Maasai of East Africa*. Oxford: Oxford University Press, 1959.

We would also like to thank all our Maasai friends, in addition to those already mentioned, who helped make the photographs possible, especially the following:

the author's brothers Naikosiai, Sambeke, and Tajewo and his sister Loiyan;

the people of Olbalbal, Tanzania, particularly Ole Pesai and his family;

the people of Loita, Kenya, and particularly Loomali Ole Koyie and his family (with special thanks to Tate and Lontini);

the families of Lengetu and Kilusu Ole Naudo of Magadi, Kenya;

Natana Ene Saitolok and Leparan Ole Paswa of Lemek, Kenya;

the warriors of Ewaso Manyatta, Kenya, with special thanks to Alaigwanani Pelela Ole Kereya and his brother Kakombe, and to Alaigwanani Makarrot Ole Nkepai;

the warriors and their girl friends, of Ewasoongidongi, Kenya, and Siyabei Manyatta, Kenya.

Finally, at Abrams, our special thanks go to Margaret Donovan for her editing, to John Lynch for his design, and, above all, to Robert Morton for his extraordinary support and creative involvement from the inception of this book.